Bugwise

Thirty Incredible Insect Investigations and Arachnid Activities

Pamela M. Hickman

Illustrations by Judie Shore

FEDERATION OF
Ontario Naturalists

Addison-Wesley Publishing Company
Reading, Massachusetts   Menlo Park, California   New York
Don Mills, Ontario   Wokingham, England   Amsterdam   Bonn
Sydney   Singapore   Tokyo   Madrid   San Juan   Paris
Seoul   Milan   Mexico City   Taipei

For my young naturalists,
Angela and Connie.
—P.H.

Principle Insect Parts

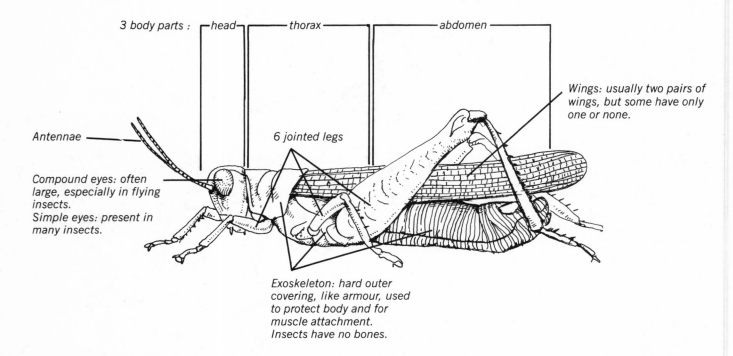

3 body parts : head — thorax — abdomen

Wings: usually two pairs of wings, but some have only one or none.

Antennae

6 jointed legs

Compound eyes: often large, especially in flying insects.
Simple eyes: present in many insects.

Exoskeleton: hard outer covering, like armour, used to protect body and for muscle attachment. Insects have no bones.

Library of Congress Cataloging-in-Publication Data

Hickman, Pamela M.
   Bugwise : thirty incredible insect investigations and arachnid activities / Pamela M. Hickman ; illustrations by Judie Shore.
      p.   cm.
   At head of title: Federation of Ontario Naturalists.
   Includes index.
   Summary: Text, illustrations, questions and answers, and suggested activities introduce the world of bugs.
   ISBN 0-201-57074-2
   1. Insects—Miscellanea—Juvenile literature.   2. Arachnida— Miscellanea—Juvenile literature. [1. Insects.]   I. Shore, Judie, ill.   II. Federation of Ontario Naturalists.   III. Title.
QL467.2.H53   1991
595.7—dc20
                                                    90-47405
                                                        CIP
                                                        AC

Text copyright © 1990 by Pamela Hickman and The Federation of Ontario Naturalists
Illustrations copyright © 1990 by Judie Shore

First published in Canada in 1990 by Kids Can Press, Ltd., Toronto, Ontario.
First published in the U.S.A. in 1991 by Addison-Wesley Publishing Company, Inc., Reading, Massachusetts.

Text and cover design by Michael Solomon
Set by Compeer Typographic Services Limited

7 8 9 10 11-CRS-0099989796
Seventh printing, June 1996

CONTENTS

Aquatic Insects

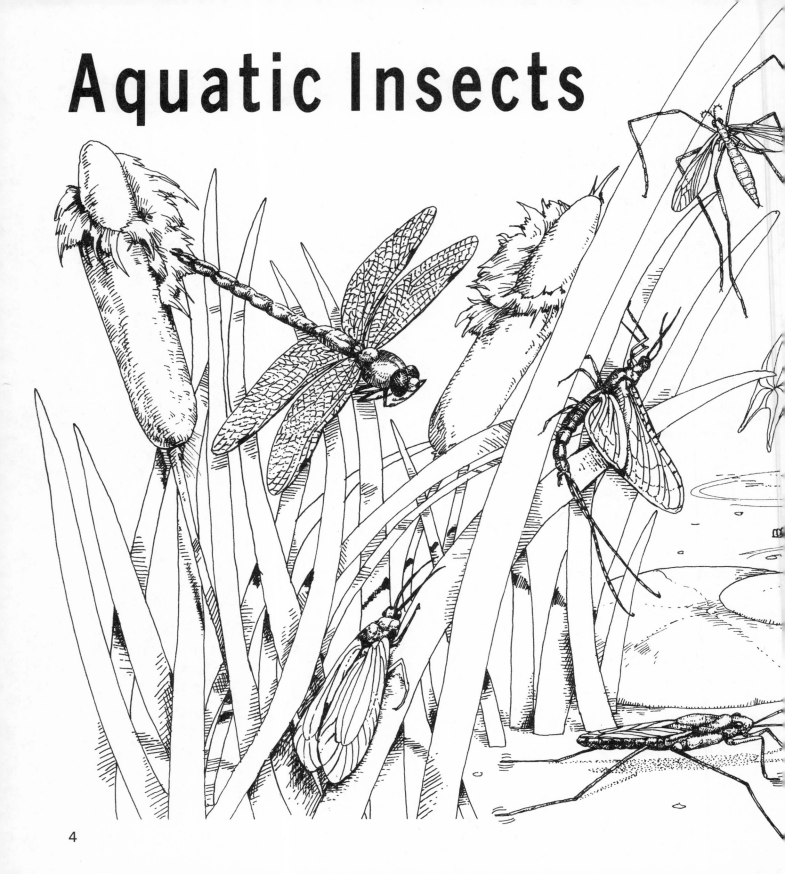

Find fresh water and you'll find insects — by the millions. In the coldest streams and the hottest hot springs, in puddles and huge lakes, insects abound.

Insects that live in water are called aquatic (ak-wah-tik). Aquatic insects live not only *in* water, but on top of the water and in the air and plants around the water. Check out the following pages and discover some of our most fascinating aquatic insects. Then head down to a local pond, stream or marsh and see who's home.

Breath-taking secrets

What do snorkellers and scuba divers have in common with mosquitoes and whirligig beetles? They all have special equipment that helps them breathe underwater. There's one big difference, though: insects' equipment is built in.

Snorkellers
How long can you hold your breath underwater? Probably not long enough to get a good look around down there. That's why many people swim with snorkels. Some insects do too. A mosquito larva has a built-in type of snorkel called a siphon at the tip of its abdomen. The larva hangs upside down from the water's surface, with the siphon sticking into the air, allowing the mosquito to take in oxygen. If the mosquito larva wants to dive, it can stay down for as long as ten minutes before running out of air. Rat-tailed maggots have a very special siphon that can be extended up to 6 cm (2½ inches), like a telescope. This lets the maggots breathe while hiding in the mud below.

Scuba divers
Unlike snorkellers, scuba divers don't have to stay near the water's surface to breathe. They take their air supply underwater with them in special tanks on their backs. Some insects have their own "tanks" to do the same thing. For instance, the giant diving beetle carries an air bubble beneath its hard outer wing covers. Unlike a scuba diver, however, the beetle doesn't have to go to the surface to replace its air supply. Where does the new supply of oxygen come from? As the oxygen in the bubble is used up, the pressure drops. This causes oxygen from the surrounding water to move into the bubble and refill the "tank."

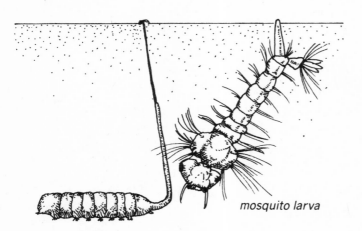

mosquito larva

rat-tailed maggot

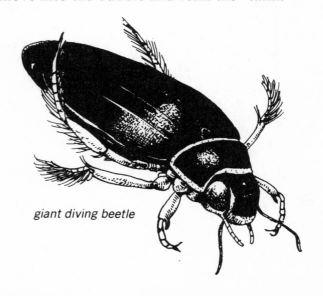

giant diving beetle

Hairy air

The water scavenger beetle has its "air tank" under its wing covers, but also traps a thin layer of air, called a plastron, on thousands of tiny hairs under its body. When it needs more air, it rises to the surface head first, tilts its head to one side and pokes an antenna through the water. Hairs on its antenna and head combine to form a funnel for air to travel down, refilling the "tank" and the plastron.

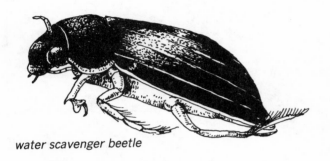

water scavenger beetle

Fishy insects

Damselflies and mayflies breathe with gills just as fish do. Their gills are at their back end and look like feathery tails. Very small insect larvae, such as chironomids, don't need gills at all. They just draw oxygen out of the water and breathe right through their skin.

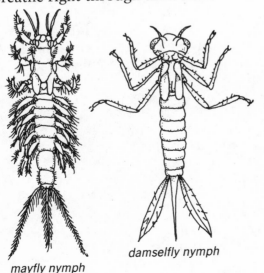

mayfly nymph

damselfly nymph

mosquito larva

Airy plants

You may have house plants. Well, some aquatic insects have plant houses. Because the stems and leaves of aquatic plants contain oxygen, what could be easier than to burrow inside for a cosy room full of air? One mosquito larva actually uses its sharp-edged siphon to saw holes into plants. Then it sucks up the oxygen just like you'd suck up a milk-shake.

7

Everything, including the kitchen sink

You've heard of fly fishing? What about fishing for flies . . . and other aquatic insects? Scrounge around the kitchen for some "tackle" and you'll be all set for one of the best fishing trips ever.

You'll need:
a shallow, light-coloured dish pan
a kitchen strainer tied to a broom handle
    for a longer reach
tweezers
a tiny paintbrush
a pail for collecting samples
a turkey baster
small, clear plastic bottles (pill bottles
    work well)
field guides to pond life, insects and
    butterflies
rubber gloves (optional — good in cold
    water)

1. Fill the dish pan with clear pond water. This will be your Home Base.
2. Dip the strainer into the pond to catch any insects swimming around. Gently jiggle your strainer around the plants, watching for any creatures that fall free.
3. Carefully transfer any finds to your Home Base using your tweezers or the paintbrush. Some insects, such as giant water bugs and water scorpions, can bite, so be careful when handling all creatures.
4. Explore the mucky bottom with your strainer and pail. Scoop up a strainer full of muck and bob it up and down in the water to wash away the silt. Look for the insects left behind and transfer them to your Home Base.

5. For a closer look at your catch, use the turkey baster to transfer insects from your dish pan to individual bottles containing water.
6. When you have finished looking at your findings and have identified them using field guides, carefully return them to their home in the pond.

Things to notice
Check out your creature's . . .
- number of legs
- colour
- size
- shape
- way of travelling
- place in the pond

Make a waterscope

Have you ever stood barefoot in a pond and felt something tickling your toes or nudging your knees? Wonder what it was? Imagine that you could shrink down to fish-size and explore the underwater world. The shrinking part may be impossible, but you *can* take a peek at the underwater world using a waterscope. With a few household items you can make this watertight spy glass and start exploring.

You'll need:
a can opener
a clean 1-L (1-quart) juice can
waterproof tape (packing or hockey tape is ideal)
clear plastic wrap
a large, strong elastic band
scissors

1. Using the can opener, remove both ends of the juice can. Carefully tape the sharp edges so you don't cut yourself.

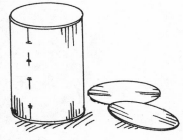

2. Stretch a piece of clear plastic wrap tightly over one end of the can, overlapping on all sides.

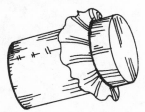

3. Put the elastic band around the end of the can so that the plastic wrap is held tightly in place.
4. Trim the edges of the plastic to make them even and then tape them down with the waterproof tape.

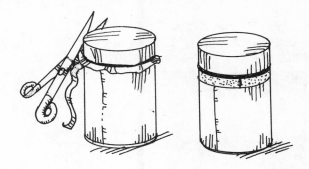

5. Test your waterscope in a basin of water. Lower the plastic-wrap end into the water, making sure that the open end never goes below the water. You look in the open end.
6. Now visit a pond or marsh and see for yourself what lurks below the water.

Waterscope down

Here's a sneak preview of what you might see when you start exploring insects underwater. Grab your new waterscope and head for the pond.

Many of these insects are still "youngsters" in the larva and nymph stages and will look very different when they get older. Turn the page to see how they've changed.

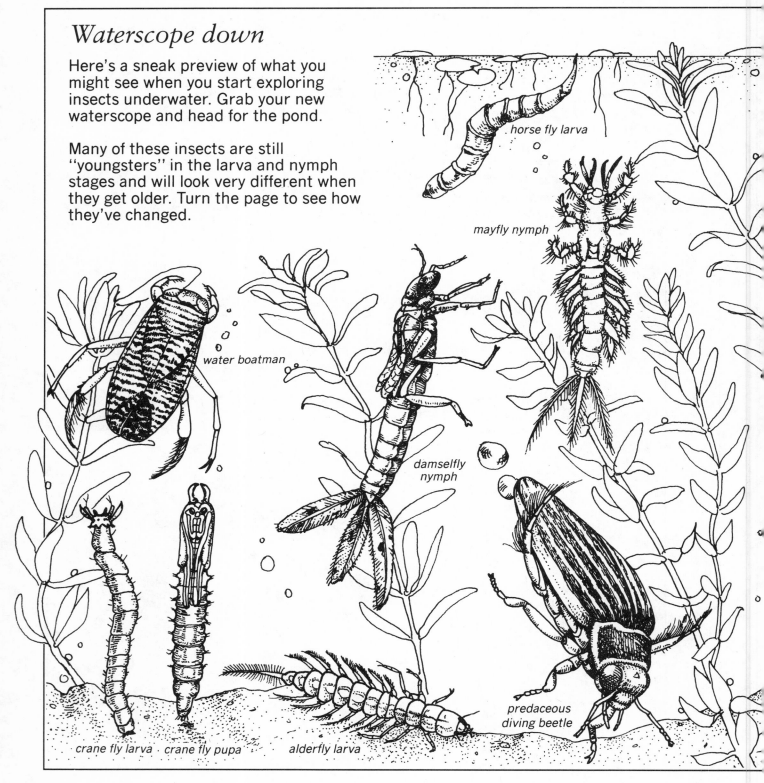

horse fly larva

mayfly nymph

water boatman

damselfly nymph

crane fly larva · crane fly pupa · alderfly larva

predaceous diving beetle

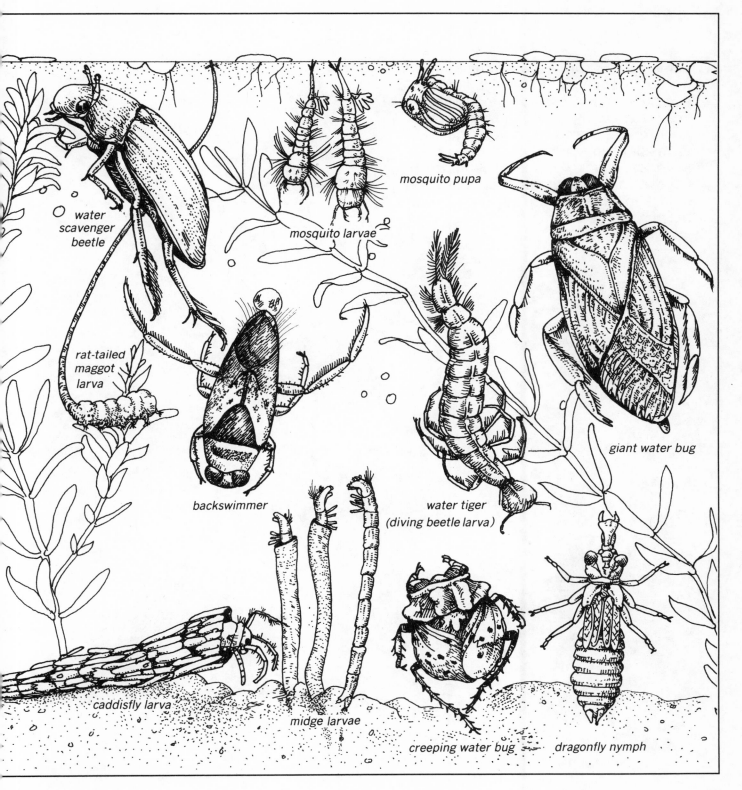

water scavenger beetle

mosquito larvae

mosquito pupa

rat-tailed maggot larva

backswimmer

water tiger (diving beetle larva)

giant water bug

caddisfly larva

midge larvae

creeping water bug

dragonfly nymph

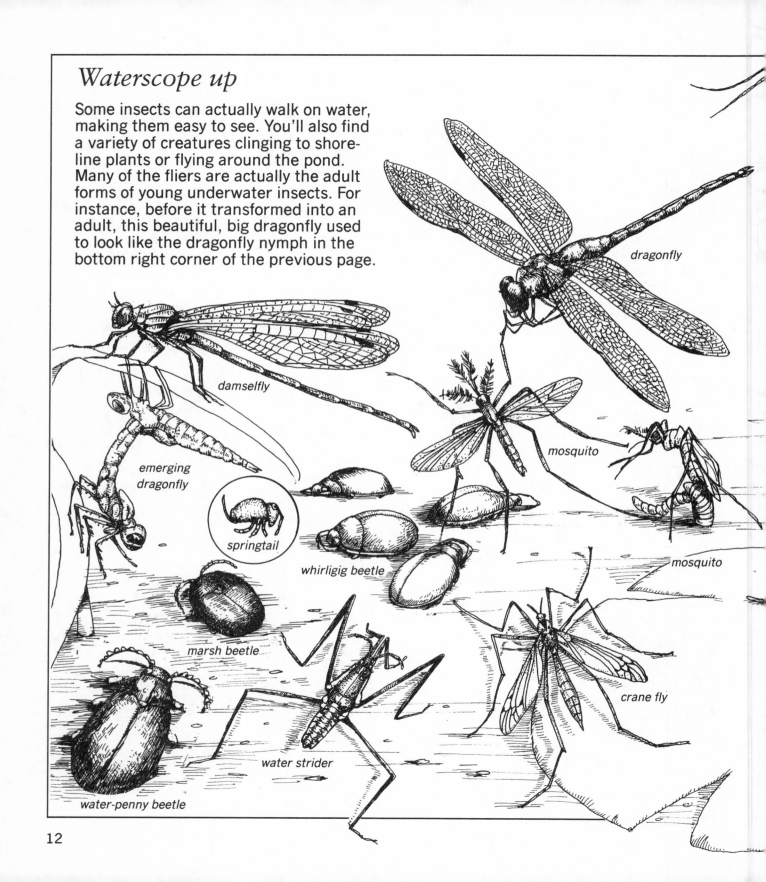

Waterscope up

Some insects can actually walk on water, making them easy to see. You'll also find a variety of creatures clinging to shoreline plants or flying around the pond. Many of the fliers are actually the adult forms of young underwater insects. For instance, before it transformed into an adult, this beautiful, big dragonfly used to look like the dragonfly nymph in the bottom right corner of the previous page.

dragonfly

damselfly

emerging dragonfly

mosquito

springtail

mosquito

whirligig beetle

marsh beetle

crane fly

water strider

water-penny beetle

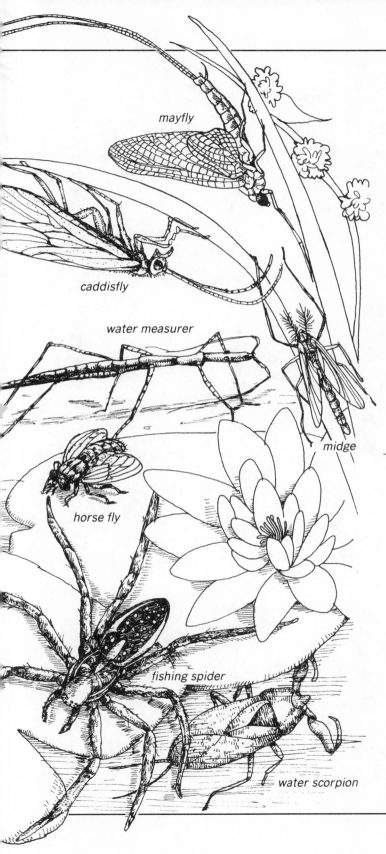

mayfly

caddisfly

water measurer

midge

horse fly

fishing spider

water scorpion

How do insects walk on water?

Wouldn't it be great to be able to walk across a pond without even getting your feet wet? Some insects can do this because of something called surface tension. Water forms a very strong, elastic-like surface where it meets the air. The water molecules "stick" tightly together and act like an invisible barrier, covering the water. You can test the strength of the water's surface with a simple trick. Fill a glass with water and very carefully lay a needle lengthwise on top of the water. Make sure you don't prick the water's surface with the needle. Even though the needle is heavier than the water, it will float as long as the surface is not penetrated.

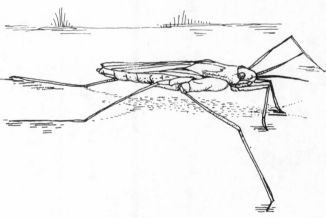

Like the needle, specially adapted aquatic insects can also stay afloat. The water strider, for example, has well-designed feet. They are covered with hairy tufts that act like snowshoes, spreading the insect's weight out over the surface so it can walk on the water. And unlike most insects, a water strider's claws are not on its feet, but part way up its legs. This prevents the claws from breaking through the surface layer.

Insects in Winter

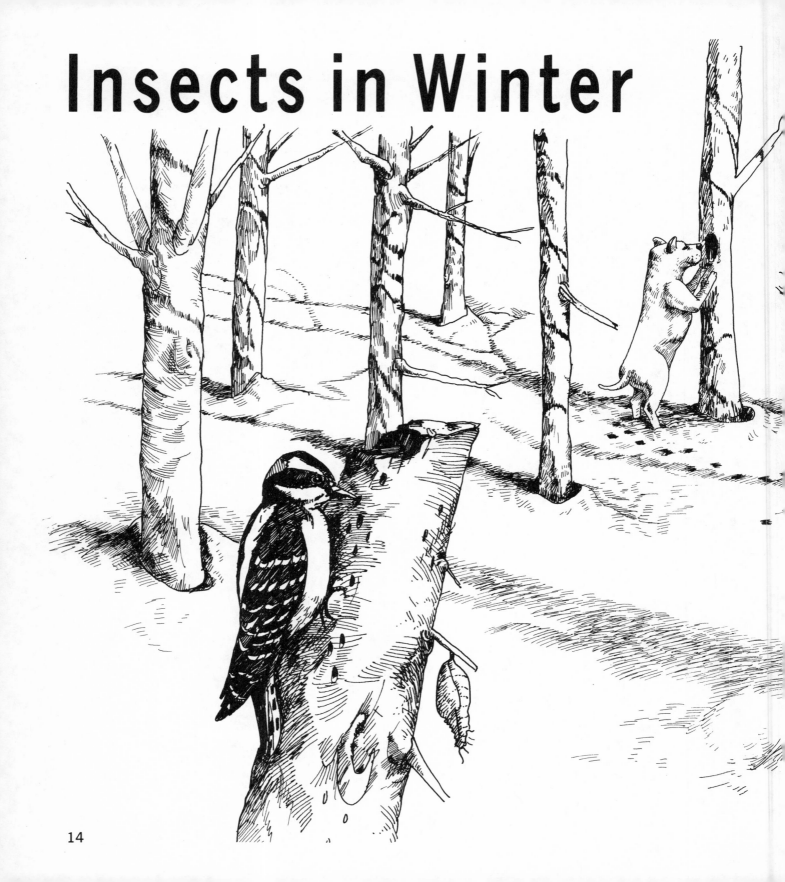

Brrr! Bundle up, brave the cold and set out to track down winter insects. You'll be surprised at how many different insects you can find when you know where to go and what to look for. Discover some of their secret hiding places and winter disguises. And when your toes and nose start tingling, you can come inside and watch a whole new insect scene inside your terrarium. With a few basic materials, you can turn bugwatching into a year-round hobby.

Watching winter insects

Have you ever gone camping in the summer? Did you go to sleep listening to the whine of mosquitoes in the tent and wake up scratching in the morning? If the bugs bugged you, try camping in the winter. It may be chilly but at least most of the bugs will be gone. Or will they?

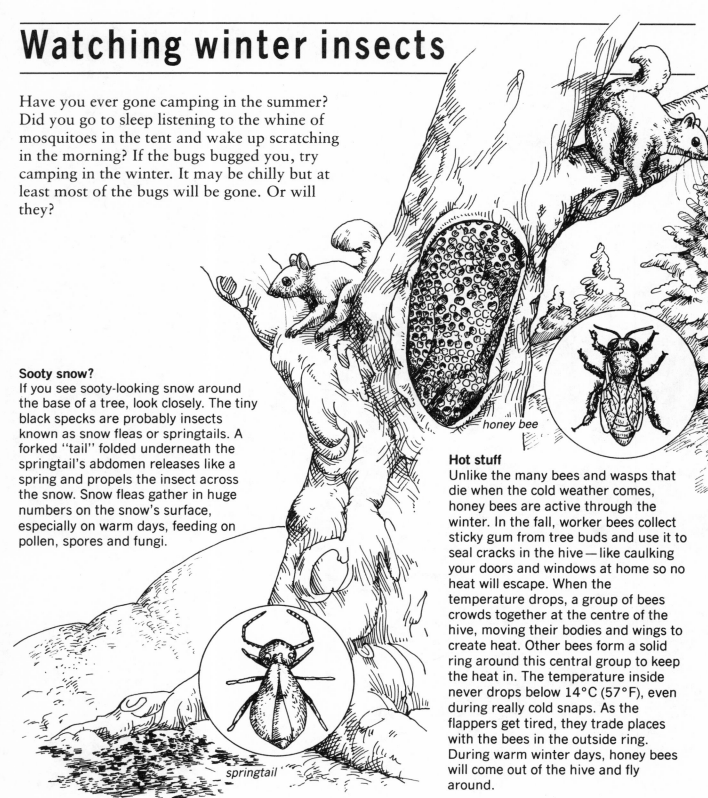

honey bee

springtail

Sooty snow?
If you see sooty-looking snow around the base of a tree, look closely. The tiny black specks are probably insects known as snow fleas or springtails. A forked "tail" folded underneath the springtail's abdomen releases like a spring and propels the insect across the snow. Snow fleas gather in huge numbers on the snow's surface, especially on warm days, feeding on pollen, spores and fungi.

Hot stuff
Unlike the many bees and wasps that die when the cold weather comes, honey bees are active through the winter. In the fall, worker bees collect sticky gum from tree buds and use it to seal cracks in the hive — like caulking your doors and windows at home so no heat will escape. When the temperature drops, a group of bees crowds together at the centre of the hive, moving their bodies and wings to create heat. Other bees form a solid ring around this central group to keep the heat in. The temperature inside never drops below 14°C (57°F), even during really cold snaps. As the flappers get tired, they trade places with the bees in the outside ring. During warm winter days, honey bees will come out of the hive and fly around.

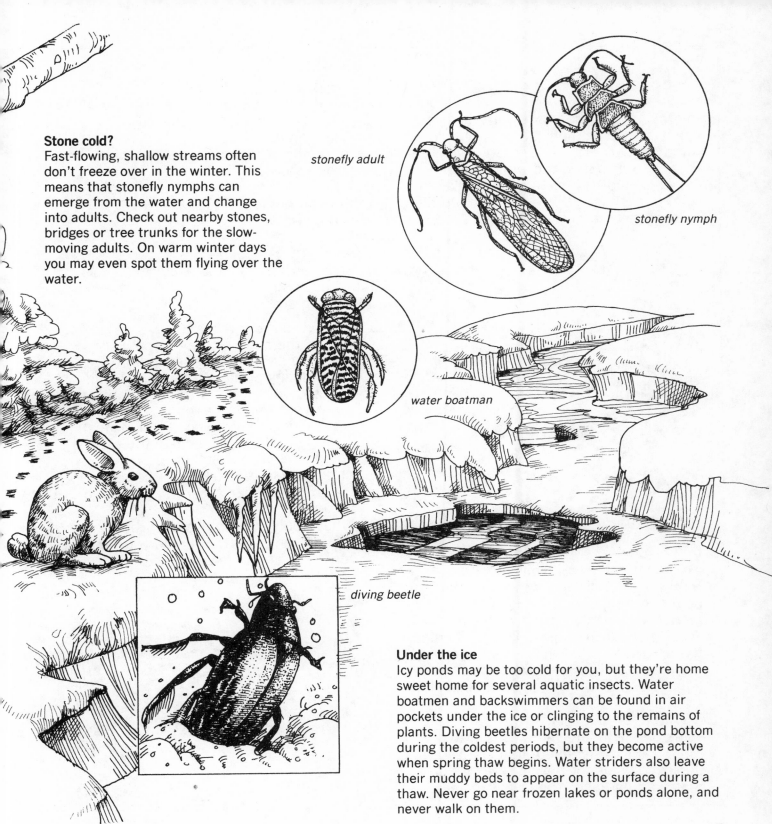

Stone cold?

Fast-flowing, shallow streams often don't freeze over in the winter. This means that stonefly nymphs can emerge from the water and change into adults. Check out nearby stones, bridges or tree trunks for the slow-moving adults. On warm winter days you may even spot them flying over the water.

stonefly adult

stonefly nymph

water boatman

diving beetle

Under the ice

Icy ponds may be too cold for you, but they're home sweet home for several aquatic insects. Water boatmen and backswimmers can be found in air pockets under the ice or clinging to the remains of plants. Diving beetles hibernate on the pond bottom during the coldest periods, but they become active when spring thaw begins. Water striders also leave their muddy beds to appear on the surface during a thaw. Never go near frozen lakes or ponds alone, and never walk on them.

17

Buried treasures

Have you ever wondered where all the moths go in the fall, or where they come from in the summer? Like many animals, moths hibernate—but not in caves like bats. Moths spend the winter inside cocoons. Moths have a cycle similar to that of butterflies. They go through four different stages:

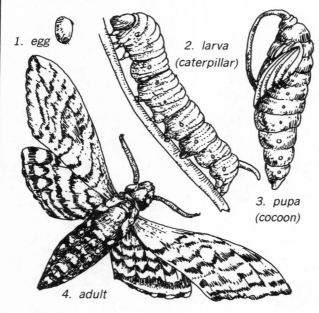

1. egg

2. larva (caterpillar)

3. pupa (cocoon)

4. adult

In the summer, adults lay their eggs which hatch into caterpillars within a few weeks. Caterpillars spend their summer doing nothing but eating. In the fall, many moth caterpillars dig into the ground and form pupae. The earth keeps them warm during winter and hides them from hungry birds and mice. Finally, in the spring, they transform into adults.

With a few materials, you can collect some pupae in late winter and watch them transform into adults in late spring. It's like digging for buried treasure and then waiting to see the jewels inside.

You'll need:
a trowel
a rinsed-out plastic tub (margarine or yoghurt) lined with cotton batting or shredded newspaper
earth or vermiculite (available at most garden stores)
water
window screening 25-30 cm (10-12 inches) wide
scissors
tape
a stick, pencil-thick, about 25 cm (10 inches) long
a foil pie plate

1. When the ground has thawed, find a tree in the open (poplar, birch, willow, beech or ash) and dig around the roots. Many pupae prefer sandy loam soil, so avoid areas with clay, stony or mucky ground. Dig about 15 cm (6 inches) down, 20-25 cm (8-10 inches) away from the north side of the tree. You should also check for pupae under any loose bark near the base of the tree and search carefully through the grass roots.

2. When you've found two or three pupae, gently place them in your lined container and carefully take them home.

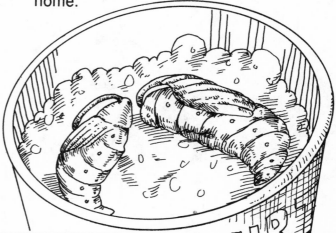

3. Cover the pupae with 3 cm (1-2 inches) of sterilized earth or vermiculite and put them in a cool place, such as a basement. (To sterilize the earth, place it on a cookie sheet in a 176°C [350°F] oven for 20 minutes.)

4. Sprinkle the soil lightly with water twice a week.

5. In late spring, check your pupae for signs of movement and changes in appearance, such as change of colour, or splitting of the pupa's skin. These are signals that the adults are ready to emerge.

6. Now roll the screen into a tube and cut it so that it stands up just on the inside edge of your container. Tape the side closed. Place the stick upright in the container and lay a pie plate over the top, to form a cage as shown.

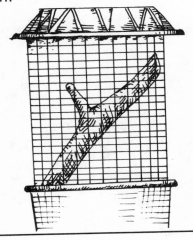

7. Keep a close eye on your treasures and you can witness one of nature's miracles. Watch as the pupa's skin splits along the back, allowing the adult to slowly climb out.

8. The adult moths will climb onto the stick and dry their wings. Inside the cocoon, the wings were tightly folded. But now that the adult can have a stretch, it pumps body fluids into the wings, making them expand into moth-size wings for flying. After a day, let your moths go free. You can keep the cocoon case as part of a collection or display.

Tricks of the trade

Nature photographers sometimes raise their own moths and butterflies. In the wild, adult insects sometimes have damaged wings or other body parts but "home-grown" specimens are usually perfect for pictures. Besides, the photographer doesn't have to search for a moth in the wild or wait hours for it to set down so a picture can be taken. Why not try photographing your pupa and adult?

Peek into a plant

Have you ever seen a goldenrod plant with a round or egg-shaped lump on its stem? These odd shapes, called galls, are not natural parts of the plant. They are caused by a fly or moth that moves in for the winter. Goldenrod galls are one of the most common galls, but many different types exist in buds, leaves, flowers, stems, twigs and even in roots of flowers, shrubs and trees.

The inside story

Goldenrod galls are formed when an adult insect lays an egg on the surface of the plant's stem. When the egg hatches, the larva (a fat, white grub) crawls along the stem, bores a hole and then crawls in. Not surprisingly, this invasion bothers the plant and it responds to the "irritation" by making extra thick layers of plant tissue around the grub. These extra layers form the gall.

Inside the gall, the larva is in insect heaven. It's surrounded by food (the plant itself), it's safe from the winter's cold and it's hidden from many predators. Living in a gall is like having a refrigerator in your cosy bedroom. Most gall insects spend winter as larvae and then change

into pupae in early spring. By early summer, a tiny adult fly or moth emerges from a little hole in the gall, completing the life cycle.

Good gall-y!

There are more than 1500 gall-making insects in North America. Even though plants and trees have no use for galls, people do. In the past, people boiled galls to extract their pigments (natural colours). These colours were used for dying wool, skin, hair and leather. Tannic acid, used in tanning and ink making, also comes from insect galls.

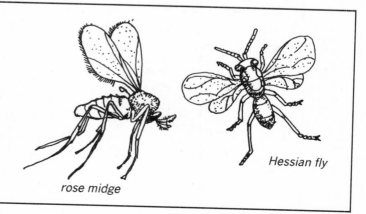

rose midge

Hessian fly

Gall collecting

Galls are fascinating mini-habitats for tiny insects and are easy to collect.

You'll need:
scissors
a bag
a pen knife
jars
screening or cheesecloth
elastic bands

1. In late summer, fall or winter, take a walk through a patch of goldenrod and collect several large round and egg-shaped galls. Use scissors to cut the stems. Place your galls in a bag. Try collecting many different galls to compare their size, shape and makers. Galls are also commonly found on oak, poplar and willow trees.

2. At home, open up a few of your galls. Ask an adult to cut them open with a sharp knife. Be careful not to damage the grub inside. If the gall is empty, look for escape holes. The gall may have been abandoned earlier in the year, or a hungry chickadee or Downy Woodpecker may have beaten you to the larva. Sometimes you'll find an unexpected resident in the gall. It may be a parasite that has killed the gall maker or a spider, bee, ant, beetle or thrip that has just moved into the empty gall.

3. Place an uncut sample of each kind of gall in jars covered with screening or with cheesecloth, tied with elastic bands.

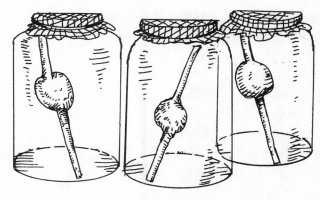

4. Put your jars in an unheated area, such as the garage or balcony, and leave them for several months. In late spring, watch for the emergence of the tiny adult insects.

Make a terrarium

Getting down on your hands and knees is a great way to find insects, especially in the woods. But when it's cold or wet you may not want to hang around very long. Instead, you can try to recreate a mini woodland habitat in your home by making a terrarium.

You'll need:
a large relish or pickle jar with a screen
  cover
pebbles or sand
small, untreated charcoal pieces
part of a rotting log
a trowel
soil dug from the woods, including leaf
  litter
water
some woodland plants and mosses from
  around the log
an elastic band

1. Turn your jar on its side. The jar's side is now the bottom of your terrarium.
2. Place a layer of small pebbles or sand on the bottom of your terrarium for drainage.

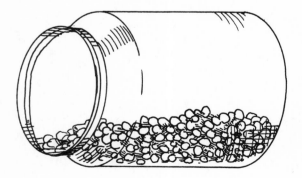

3. Sprinkle a thin layer of charcoal pieces over the sand to keep the soil fresh.

4. Take your terrarium to the woods and find a small rotting log, full of life. Remember, you can't dig in parks, conservation areas or nature reserves. If you're on private land, be sure to get permission first. Take only a few specimens so you don't disturb the area too much.
5. Add the soil and leaf litter from around the rotting log to your terrarium so that it is 5-7 cm (2-3 inches) thick.

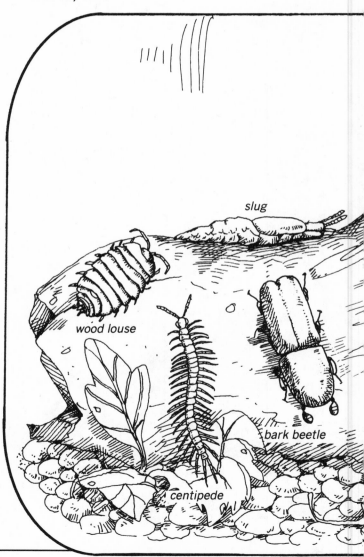

slug

wood louse

bark beetle

centipede

6. Moisten this mixture slightly and shape it into small hills to simulate the natural ups and downs of the forest floor.
7. Carefully break off a piece of the rotting log and place it in your terrarium. Take as large a piece as will fit, but don't squish it in.

8. Dig up some of the mosses and small woodland plants growing around the log. Place them in your terrarium as they grew in the wild. Press the plants down firmly and dampen them with water. Your terrarium should be kept moist but not soaked.
9. Place the screen over the jar mouth and secure it with the elastic band.
10. At home, place your container in an area where it will get some natural sunlight, fresh air and temperatures between 18 and 24°C (65 and 75°F). Avoid too much direct sunlight, dry heat or draughts. Place heavy objects, such as two big books, in front of and behind your terrarium to keep it from rolling.
11. When you're finished with your terrarium, be sure to return the creatures to their original homes when the weather is warm again.

Take note
Keep a pencil and notebook near your terrarium so you can jot down interesting events. Try to make a list or sketch of all of the creatures you see. When looking at your mini-world, try to answer these questions:

☐ *What is the colour, size, shape, number of legs, etc. of each animal?*
☐ *Where do the different creatures live?*
☐ *Do they move around or stay in one place?*
☐ *How do they move?*
☐ *Are they more active at certain times of day or night?*
☐ *What do they eat?*
☐ *What do the animals use the plants and soil for?*

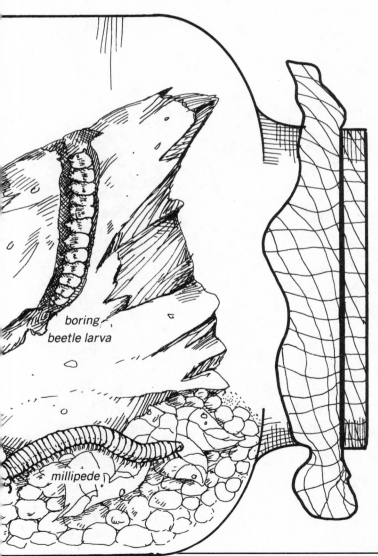

boring beetle larva

millipede

Flies inside

"Buzz, buzz, thwack, buzz, buzz." Can you guess what that is? It's the familiar sound of a frustrated house fly caught inside a window. When the warm weather arrives, house flies that have spent the winter in your walls or attic try to make their escape. Most people are only too happy to see them go. Before you say goodbye, look for these nifty fly features.

Neat feet

Have you ever wondered how flies walk upside-down on the ceiling without falling off? Each of their six feet is specially equipped with a pair of small claws that helps them cling to rough surfaces. But, how do flies walk on smooth glass? Under each claw are two tiny pads covered in hairs that release a glue-like substance so flies can stick to glass or ceilings without tumbling down.

Flies flying

Flies are great fliers. House flies beat their wings 11 000 times per minute and can fly an average speed of 8 km/h (5 mph). It's the fast wing beats that produce the buzzing sound you hear when a fly flies by. Unlike butterflies or dragonflies, flies have only one pair of wings. Instead of hind wings, they have little rods called halteres on their thorax that act as stabilizers during flight and keep them flying level.

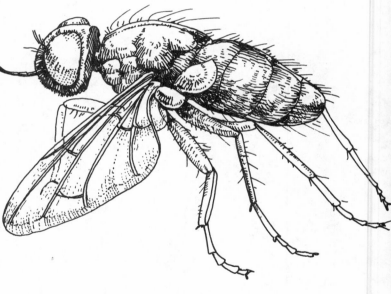

Have you ever noticed the little black lines all over a fly's wings? These are veins. Just as your veins carry blood to various parts of your body, the fly's veins take blood to its wings, but they also do other things. When the adult emerges from its pupa, air is pumped through the veins to help the folded wings expand. The veins also strengthen the wings and provide support, just as the cross-pieces on a kite keep the kite from collapsing.

A fly's eyes

If you held a colander up to your face and looked through it, you'd see many tiny holes aimed in slightly different directions. This is just what the compound eyes of flies and other insects are like. Instead of having only one lens in each eye, like you, each house fly's eye has 4000 tiny lenses in individual six-sided facets. Each facet is like each hole in the colander—pointing at a slightly different angle and seeing a small part of a total picture. When all of the tiny parts are put together, the insect sees a

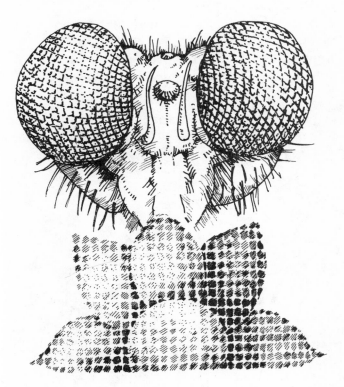

mosaic-like image. The more facets, the clearer the picture. Although compound eyes sound like super seers, they don't work as well as your eyes. Insects can't focus their eyes so, although they can see movement very well, images are not clear beyond 1 m (2-3 feet). And with no eyelids, insects have to keep their eyes open day and night—even when they sleep.

"Flies in the sugar-bowl, two by two . . ."

The flies in your sugar-bowl aren't "skipping to my Lou," they're probably tasting the sugar—with their feet! Can you imagine wading barefoot across a pizza? A fly can tell if food is worth eating, just by walking on it. But since a fly's mouth is designed only to soak up liquids, it can't just eat your sugar. First, it spits saliva onto it to make the food liquidy, and then it sucks up the sweet treat like a sponge.

Fly facts

- [ ] *The expression "breeding like flies" comes from flies' fantastic ability to multiply. Each female house fly produces about 1000 eggs in only a few weeks.*

- [ ] *Don't let the combing and cleaning routine of the fly on your table fool you. A single house fly can carry millions of germs inside and outside of its body.*

Winter disguises

Some insects spend the winter as eggs, others as larvae, pupae or even adults. Each stage has its own advantages for winter survival.

Eggs are surprisingly good at resisting the cold. Some mosquito eggs are even adapted to hatch in the water left by melting snow.

Larvae that are well hidden and surrounded by food, such as the grubs inside galls, can eat and grow through the winter.

Pupae, such as the cocoons of moths, don't feed at all during winter but spend the time waiting to turn into an adult in spring. The sealed cocoon helps protect the insect inside from bad weather and hungry predators.

Mourning cloak butterflies and some other insects hibernate as adults, allowing them to mate and start a family very early in spring.

Where to look
You can find insects hibernating just about anywhere in winter. Some spend winter underground; others hide under stones, rocks, rotting logs, bark, leaves and man-made structures such as porches, siding and shingles. A few sneaky insects try to move inside your home for a nice warm winter.

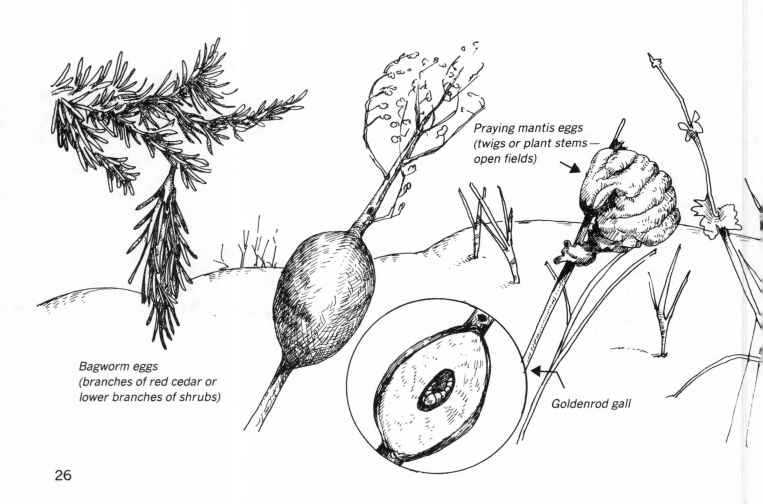

*Bagworm eggs
(branches of red cedar or
lower branches of shrubs)*

*Praying mantis eggs
(twigs or plant stems —
open fields)*

Goldenrod gall

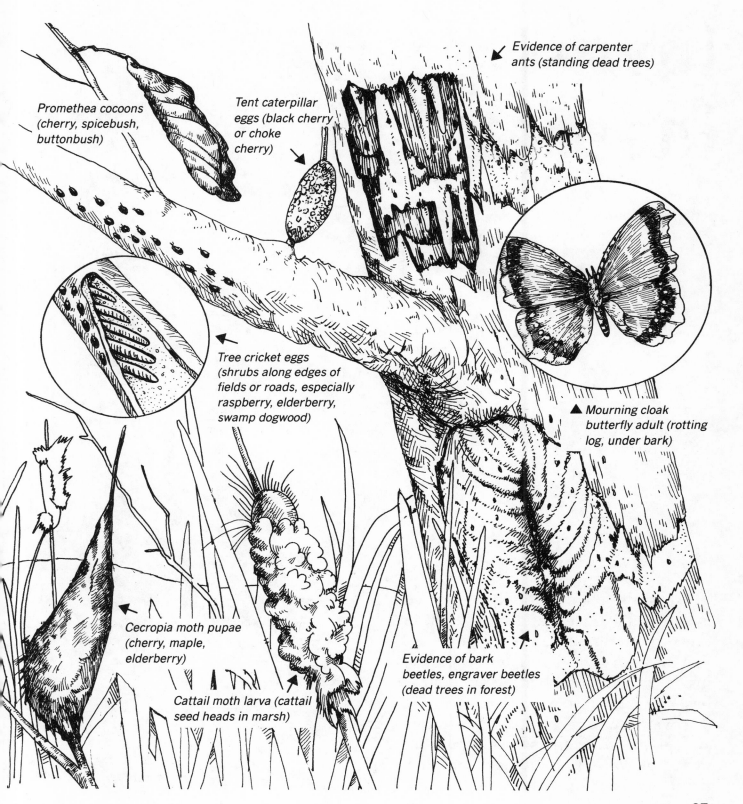

Promethea cocoons
(cherry, spicebush,
buttonbush)

Tent caterpillar
eggs (black cherry
or choke
cherry)

Evidence of carpenter
ants (standing dead trees)

Tree cricket eggs
(shrubs along edges of
fields or roads, especially
raspberry, elderberry,
swamp dogwood)

▲ Mourning cloak
butterfly adult (rotting
log, under bark)

Cecropia moth pupae
(cherry, maple,
elderberry)

Cattail moth larva (cattail
seed heads in marsh)

Evidence of bark
beetles, engraver beetles
(dead trees in forest)

Investigating Insects

The best thing about looking for insects is that you'll always find some—they're everywhere. Insects even live in places you may never have thought to look—inside leaves, under bark, or in your basement, for instance. Read on and discover how you can spend your time sweeping, sifting and searching for an incredible variety of flipping, flopping, flying and hopping insects.

Bugwatching clothes

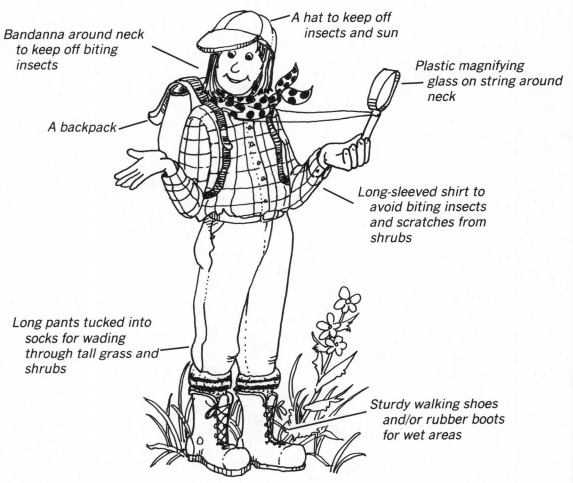

Bandanna around neck to keep off biting insects

A hat to keep off insects and sun

Plastic magnifying glass on string around neck

A backpack

Long-sleeved shirt to avoid biting insects and scratches from shrubs

Long pants tucked into socks for wading through tall grass and shrubs

Sturdy walking shoes and/or rubber boots for wet areas

Bugwatching bring-alongs

A few bugwatching tools can help you discover a whole world of hidden surprises.

☐ *lunch/snacks for you*
☐ *bug catcher for catching insects without harming them (see box on page 31)*
☐ *bug box — This is a small clear plastic box that has a magnifying lens set in the removable lid. You can put an insect in the box to watch it, and then set it free. These are available at most science or nature supply stores. You can make one by using a clear plastic pill bottle and resting a small plastic magnifying glass over the top as a lid to look through.*
☐ *tweezers for picking up insects*
☐ *insect repellent to keep the biters from biting*
☐ *field guides (insects, beetles, butterflies, moths and pond life)*
☐ *pad and pencil for making notes or sketches*

Make a bug catcher

What do you get when you cross a baby-food jar with two drinking straws? A terrific bug catcher, of course!

You'll need:
a hammer
a large nail
a jar lid
2 flexible bendable drinking straws or
   pieces of plastic aquarium tubing
tape
a small piece of cheesecloth
a small glass jar, like a baby-food jar

1. Hammer the nail into the lid to make two holes, 0.5 cm (¼ inch) wide each, and about 3 cm (1 inch) apart.
2. Turn the lid over and hammer down the sharp edges around the holes.
3. Push the two straws or tubes through the holes in the jar lid. Use tape, to seal around them.
4. Tape a piece of cheesecloth over the bottom of one tube. This is to prevent you sucking insects into your mouth.
5. Place the lid tightly on the jar.
6. To catch a bug, place the tube with the cheesecloth attached at the bottom in your mouth and suck hard. Place the open end of the other tube near a small insect. The insect will be sucked through the tube and into your jar. Now you can have a good look at it before letting it go.

Make a bug hat

For really buggy days, keep the flies out of your face with this easy-to-make bug hat.

You'll need:
mosquito netting
a hat
a needle
thread
scissors

1. Cut a length of mosquito netting wide enough to extend around the brim of your hat plus 5 cm (2 inches) extra, and about 35 cm (14 inches) long.
2. Sew the ends of your netting together with a 3 cm (1 inch) seam to form a tube.
3. Sew one end of the tube to the brim of your hat. Your stitches should be close together so there are no gaps where insects can sneak in.
4. Put on your hat and tuck the free end of the netting into the collar of your shirt.

Take a hike

What better way to find out about insects in your neighbourhood than by going on an insect hike? You can find out where lacewings live, how caterpillars crawl or what earwigs eat. So, get dressed for bugwatching and let's go.

Theme hikes
How about a dragonfly hike or a grasshopper hike? If you have favourite insects, focus an outing on them. Find out what habitat they prefer and head for it. For example, dragonflies dance along the edges of ponds and streams, but grasshoppers go for long grass and wildflower meadows. When you're concentrating on only one or two kinds of insects at a time, you will be able to spend more time learning how to identify them. You can watch for features such as colour, size and wing shape and begin to recognize different species.

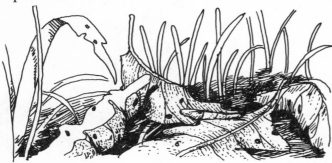

Some states have check-lists for certain insects, such as butterflies, that list all the species of butterflies that have been found in a particular area. When you identify a butterfly, you can check the list to make sure the butterfly is really found in the area where you saw it. Contact your state nature organization or local natural history museum to see if they have any check-lists you can use.

Mini-hikes
Who said hikes have to be long, or even on foot? Take a mini-hike and give your feet a rest. Try crawling around on your hands and knees, taking time to really look at the ground for those well-hidden bugs. Or, let your fingers do the walking. Find a rotting log and probe and poke your way through it with your hands and a pair of tweezers. Take a mini-hike on a tree. Start at ground level and work your way up, checking in the grooves of bark, under loose bark, in holes, in buds, on and under leaves and in blossoms, seeds, cones or nuts. You can hike for hours and never get sore feet!

Tricks of the trade

Many insects prefer quiet, dark places and take a bit of persuasion to come into the open. Here are a few "tricks of the trade" for finding insects and luring them out into the open.

Low life

Ground-dwelling insects may come out of hiding if you tempt them with a sweet and sticky snack.

You'll need:

a trowel
a rinsed-out soup can with one end
    removed
a spoon
peanut butter and jam.

1. In a field or woods, dig a hole big enough to hold your can. Pack soil around the can, making sure the open end is level with the ground.
2. Put a couple of spoonfuls of jam in the can and spread a thin layer of peanut butter around the inside of the rim.

3. Leave your trap for several hours or overnight, and then come back to see what you've caught.
4. After you've had a good look at your guests, let them go. Remove your can and fill in the hole. Try placing your can in a different habitat and compare the kinds and numbers of creatures that you catch.

Shake it, baby, shake it!

Small shrubs are super hiding places for insects. Wherever they're clinging, you can shake them out to get a closer look. Take an old white or light-coloured sheet and spread it on the ground underneath a shrub. Give the bush a good shake. You should find that several different kinds of creatures have dropped on to your sheet. When you're through looking, leave them near the bottom of the bush and they will climb or fly back up.

Peek-a-boo

When out for a walk, play a game of peek-a-boo with the wildlife. Many insects and other animals shelter under stones, rocks and rotting logs. Carefully lift up these hiding places to reveal the life hiding below. If you're lucky, you'll find various beetles, ants, wood lice, centipedes, millipedes, slugs, snails, earthworms and maybe even a salamander. Don't forget to replace the stones or logs where they were so the animals will be protected.

Busy bees (and wasps)

You may not want a bee in your bonnet, but a bee's nest in your neighbourhood can be fascinating. There are more than 3300 species of bees and wasps in North America, so you're bound to discover some of their amazing nests. Afraid of being told to buzz off by a busy bee? Just wait until winter when most nest owners have been killed by the cold. Even if the nest is active, with bees or wasps moving in and out, you can keep a safe distance and still identify the owners by the shape of their nest. Here's a mini-guide to some of the most common nests. Try to match the nests to the owners below. (Answers on page 96.)

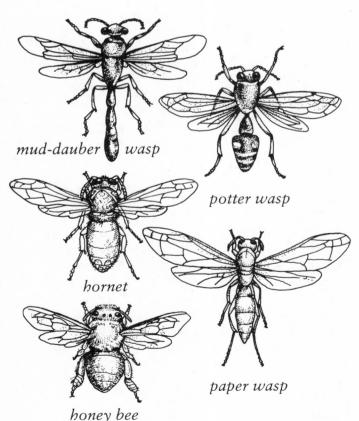

mud-dauber wasp

potter wasp

hornet

paper wasp

honey bee

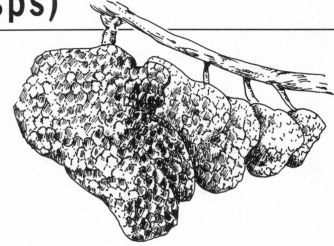

Wax works
Hundreds of other workers and I spend our days making six-sided cells out of beeswax and gluing thousands of cells together to make honeycombs. You can find our nests in holes, hollow trees or rock crevices, but you may also see our honeycombs hanging in the open from a tree branch. What am I?

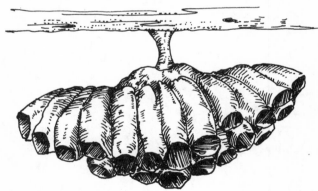

Paper nests
I've been making pulp and paper much longer than people. By chewing up the stringy fibres of rotting wood or plant stems and mixing it with saliva, I produce a pulp-like material. This is shaped into a single layer of open-ended cells that looks like papier-mâché when dry. My nest hangs by a short stalk beneath eaves, porches and other overhangs. What am I?

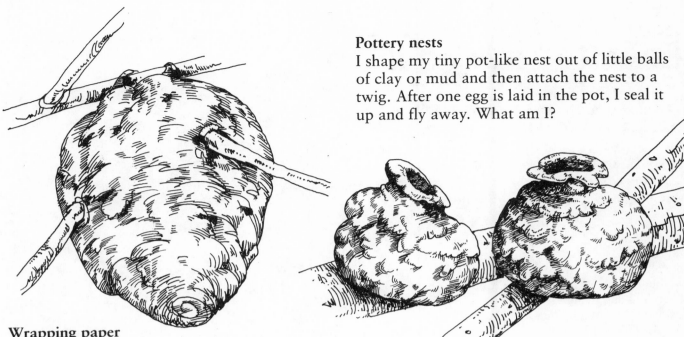

Pottery nests

I shape my tiny pot-like nest out of little balls of clay or mud and then attach the nest to a twig. After one egg is laid in the pot, I seal it up and fly away. What am I?

Wrapping paper

My paper nest hangs from trees, shrubs or the eaves of buildings. As the queen, I started the nest as one cell, but it got bigger and bigger as more workers were born to help me. The outside of my nest is wrapped up in sheets of paper, like a Christmas present. The only door is a small hole at the bottom or side. What am I?

Breakfast in bed

Instead of flying back and forth to feed their hungry babies, some wasp mothers are really organized. A female potter wasp hunts down caterpillars, stings them and then stuffs the paralyzed insects into her tiny, pot-shaped nest before laying an egg inside. When her larva hatches, it has all the food it needs, without having to get out of bed.

Organ pipes

In sheltered spots like eaves, sheds or bridges, you'll find my long, tubular nests made from balls of mud. People think my nests look like organ pipes. What am I?

Look for life on a leaf

The next time you jump into a pile of leaves, take a closer look at what you've landed in. If there are oak, poplar, birch or fruit tree leaves in your pile, you're in for a surprise. Your leaves provide food and homes for a variety of tiny insects. Here are a few things to look for.

Leaf miners

If your leaf has small see-through blotches in it, like tiny windows, or a winding maze of trails, it has probably been invaded by leaf miners. The larvae of leaf-mining flies, beetles, wasps, butterflies and moths are so tiny that they can burrow into the space between the upper and lower surfaces of a leaf. They eat the soft leaf tissue (the green part) and leave the stringy bits behind. Insects that wander while they eat create a system of tiny pathways that show you where they've been.

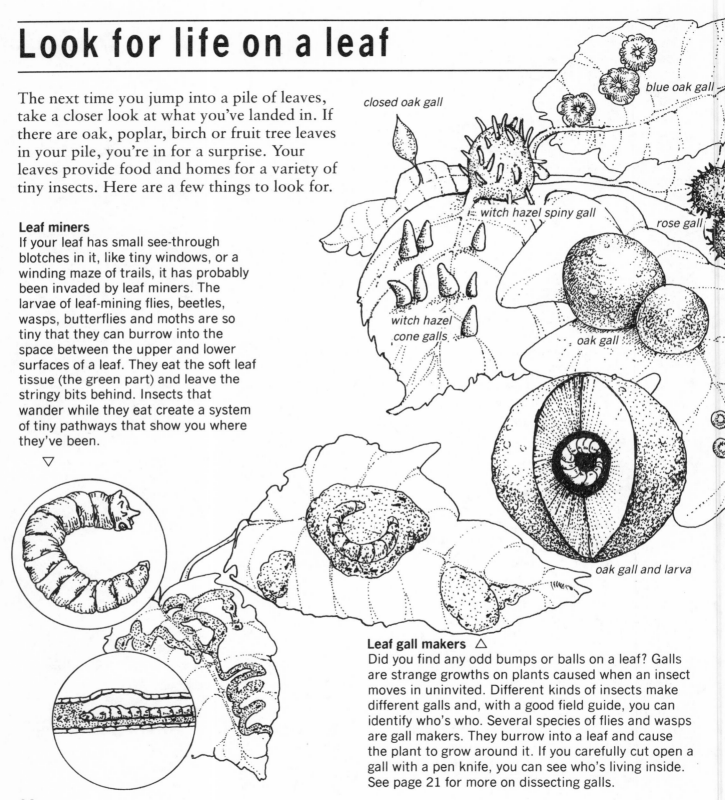

closed oak gall

blue oak gall

witch hazel spiny gall

rose gall

witch hazel cone galls

oak gall

oak gall and larva

Leaf gall makers △

Did you find any odd bumps or balls on a leaf? Galls are strange growths on plants caused when an insect moves in uninvited. Different kinds of insects make different galls and, with a good field guide, you can identify who's who. Several species of flies and wasps are gall makers. They burrow into a leaf and cause the plant to grow around it. If you carefully cut open a gall with a pen knife, you can see who's living inside. See page 21 for more on dissecting galls.

Lunching on leaves

If you've found some leaves with big holes eaten out of them, take a closer look—the munchers may still be around. Caterpillars of moths and butterflies are often found lunching on leaves. One of the most common is the inchworm—a smooth, thin caterpillar that moves by arching its body and pulling its back end forward to meet its front end. ▽

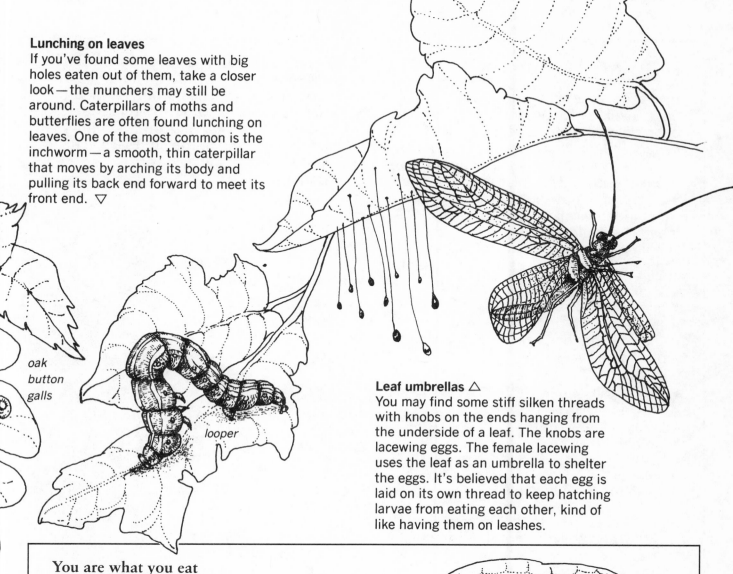

oak button galls

looper

Leaf umbrellas △

You may find some stiff silken threads with knobs on the ends hanging from the underside of a leaf. The knobs are lacewing eggs. The female lacewing uses the leaf as an umbrella to shelter the eggs. It's believed that each egg is laid on its own thread to keep hatching larvae from eating each other, kind of like having them on leashes.

You are what you eat

Imagine if you ate tomatoes and turned red, or carrots and turned orange? Cutworms actually turn green after filling up on juicy green leaves. And monarch butterfly larvae absorb chemicals from the milkweed plants that they eat. The chemicals are stored in the butterfly's body and make the monarch taste very bad to its predators. Birds soon learn to avoid the awful tasting black and orange butterflies. So, by eating milkweed, monarchs not only get fed, but they also get built-in protection from their enemies.

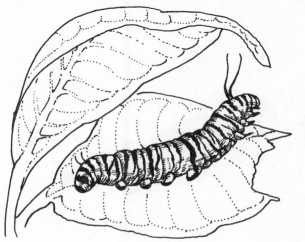

Nature's recyclers

Everyone's recycling these days. It may be a new idea for people, but nature has been doing it ever since life on earth began. In fact, there are millions of tiny plants and animals that spend their lives breaking down dead plants and animals into reusable nutrients. Without these well-hidden workers, our forests and meadows couldn't grow. With some simple equipment, you can discover some of these recyclers in a small sample of soil.

You'll need:
a shovel
some soil and leaf litter from the woods
a plastic bag
wire cutters
stiff wire screening with large holes
a funnel
a damp paper towel
a wide-mouth jar
a light
tweezers
a small magnifying glass

1. Use the shovel to dig up some leaf litter and soil and put it in the plastic bag.

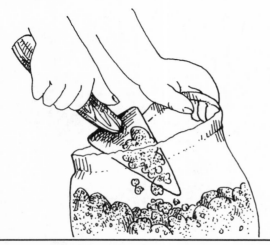

2. At home, set up your equipment. Cut the screen to fit inside the funnel, about 6 cm (2 inches) from the mouth. Place the damp paper towel in the bottom of your jar and set the funnel in the open end of the jar. Place your light so that it shines directly over the funnel.

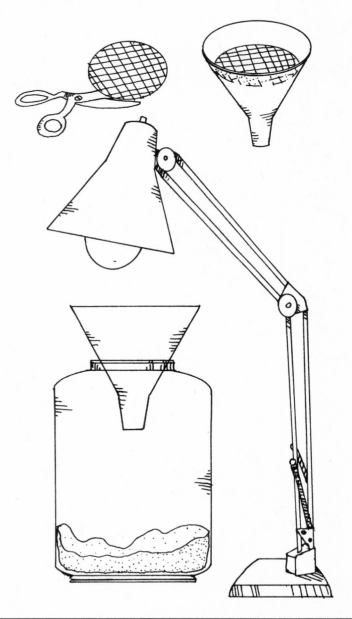

3. Put the soil in your funnel and turn on the light. The rest of the room should be dark.

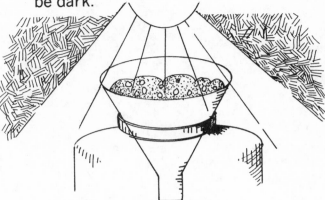

4. Leave the equipment set up overnight. The creatures in your sample will try to get away from the heat and light of your lamp by burrowing deeper into the soil. Eventually they will fall through the funnel, into the jar below.

5. Gently pick up each creature with the tweezers so you can get a closer look with your magnifying glass.

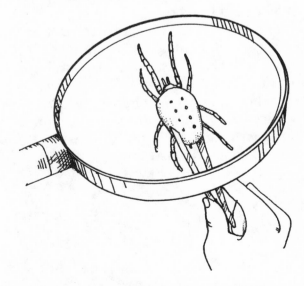

6. When you've finished, return the animals and soil to their habitat.

What you'll find

You'll probably find a variety of insects and non-insects in your soil. Here are a few to look for:

Insects:

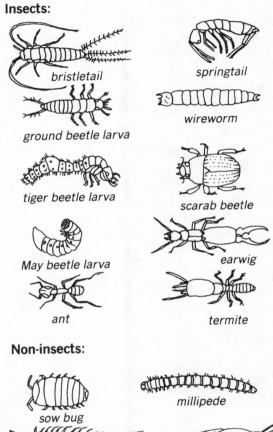

bristletail

springtail

ground beetle larva

wireworm

tiger beetle larva

scarab beetle

May beetle larva

earwig

ant

termite

Non-insects:

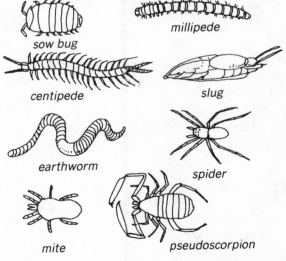

sow bug

millipede

centipede

slug

earthworm

spider

mite

pseudoscorpion

The music makers

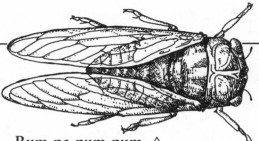

Some people have to carry instruments as big as a tuba or cello in order to make music. But musical insects are lucky—their "instruments" are built in. They make music simply by playing different parts of their bodies.

Insect music is usually played by males that are trying to attract mates. Male crickets, however, also chirp to defend their territories. Scientists have discovered that all insects sing more slowly as the temperature drops. The snowy tree cricket has been called a "living thermometer" because of its very regular rate of chirping. In fact, if you count the number of chirps in eight seconds and add four, you'll have the approximate temperature in Celsius. (For Fahrenheit, count the chirps in 15 seconds and add 37.)

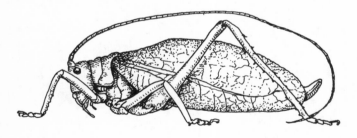

Hey diddle diddle △
A violin makes music when the bow is drawn over the strings. Some insects do this too. They have a row of bumps known as a file and they have a scraper, which is a ridge or knob sticking out from part of their wings. By rubbing the file and scraper together, the insect produces a sound. Chirpers such as crickets and katydids make their music by rapidly rubbing the file (really a raised vein) on one wing against the scraper on another wing. Katydids may rub their wings together up to 50 million times in one summer!

Rum-pa-pum-pum △
Male cicadas are the loudest of all insects, broadcasting up to 400 m (440 yards) away, especially on hot summer days. Cicadas are sometimes called hydro bugs because their buzzing-like noise sounds like the vibrations from heavy power lines or fluorescent lights. Their sound is produced from a pair of drum-like membranes (drumheads) on their abdomens. Inside the abdomen's air chamber is a group of muscles attached to the drumhead. By tightening the muscles, the drumhead is tensed, like pulling back on an elastic band. When the muscles are relaxed, the drumhead vibrates, hitting the inside of the abdomen's walls and producing the familiar sound.

Whiners and buzzers
Lie in a field on a warm summer's day with your eyes closed and you'll soon hear the sounds of insects. Listen for the whining of mosquitoes and buzzing of bees. How do they make their sounds? The beating of their wings produces the music—the faster the wing beat, the higher the pitch. Which one do you think beats its wings the fastest?

Clickers . . .

Have you ever turned a beetle over on its back? It wiggles its legs in the air but can't get flipped over again. The click beetle is an exception; it has a built in catapult. Its flexible body arches and then suddenly straightens up. As it straightens, a small, spring-like peg on its abdomen is released, launching the beetle into the air and producing a loud clicking noise.

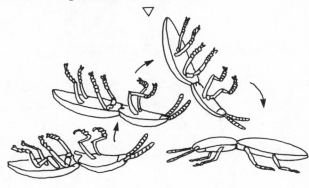

. . . and tickers

You've heard of a haunted house, but what about a haunted chair or desk? Death-watch beetles burrow into wood and make a ticking sound inside their burrows by knocking their head against the wood to call a mate. Superstitious people believed that the ticking sound was a forewarning of death.

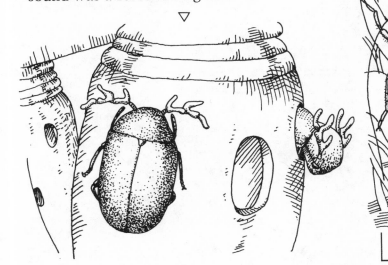

A private concert

In Japan, some people keep cicadas and crickets in cages so they can listen to them sing.

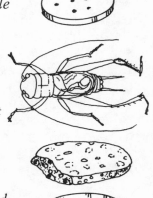

You can collect and keep an adult cricket in a jar in your own home. Put a wet sponge in the jar to give your temporary pet moisture and feed it ground-up dry dog food or chicken mash.

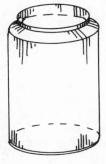

Be sure to punch holes in the jar's lid with a hammer and nail. Not only will you enjoy your cricket's serenades, but you will also be able to see how it makes its music. You can even try to catch a snowy tree cricket and see how accurately it can tell the temperature. Be sure to return the cricket to its natural home by late fall.

41

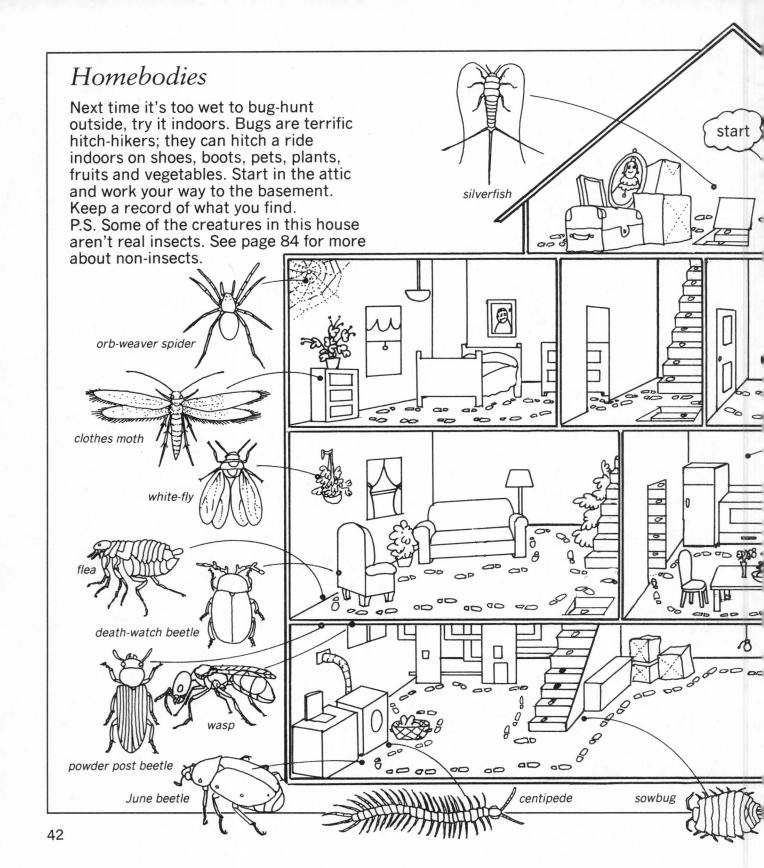

Homebodies

Next time it's too wet to bug-hunt outside, try it indoors. Bugs are terrific hitch-hikers; they can hitch a ride indoors on shoes, boots, pets, plants, fruits and vegetables. Start in the attic and work your way to the basement. Keep a record of what you find.

P.S. Some of the creatures in this house aren't real insects. See page 84 for more about non-insects.

silverfish

start

orb-weaver spider

clothes moth

white-fly

flea

death-watch beetle

powder post beetle

wasp

June beetle

centipede

sowbug

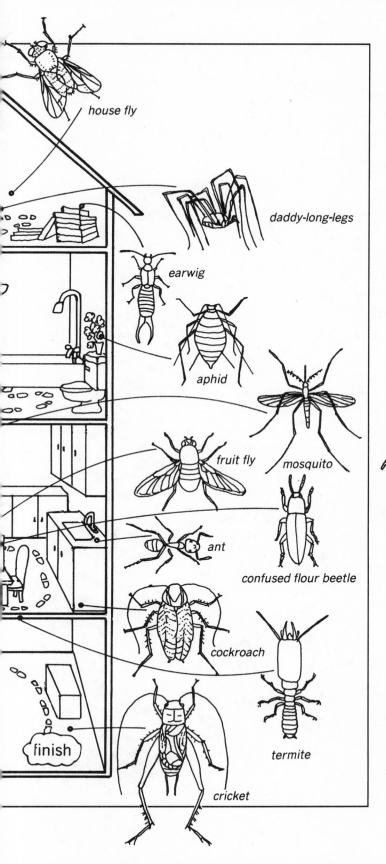

house fly

daddy-long-legs

earwig

aphid

fruit fly

mosquito

confused flour beetle

ant

cockroach

termite

cricket

finish

Bug off!
Tired of swatting and missing? Try some of these unusual ways to get bugs to bug off.

☐ Hang sprigs of mint in doorways to keep flies out.

☐ Catch a few ladybugs and put them on your houseplants to control aphids.

☐ Grow tansy outside your kitchen wall to keep ants away.

☐ Encourage toads in your garden. One toad can eat up to 10 000 insects in just three months. In fact, before insect sprays were invented, some people kept toads indoors to control bugs.

☐ Grow insect-repelling plants, such as marigolds, asters, chrysanthemums, nasturtiums, cosmos, coreopsis and coriander.

☐ Attract insect-eating birds to your garden by providing bird houses, bird baths, shrubs and trees for shelter.

Insects on the go

When you were a baby learning to walk, you had to try really hard to move your legs without falling over. Imagine what it would have been like with six legs? When insects walk, they usually have three legs on the ground (one on one side and two on the other) and three legs in motion—now *that* would take practice. But insects do a lot more than just walk. They flap, hover, glide, jump, climb, dive, swim, row and even burrow.

Jumping

Crickets, grasshoppers, springtails, leafhoppers and fleas are all terrific jumpers. In fact, a common flea can jump about 10 000 times per hour without getting tired.

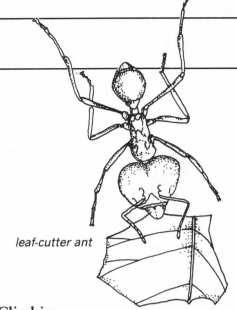

leaf-cutter ant

Climbing

Could you climb up and down a huge mountain every day? Leaf-cutter ants are less than 3 cm (1 inch) long but they climb 60 m (200 feet) trees daily. They can even carry their own weight in leaves all the way back down. That would be like climbing down a mountain while carrying a friend.

Burrowing

Getting around underground is important too, especially if you're a mole cricket. It has specially designed strong, flattened front legs that act as shovels and rakes for moving soil.

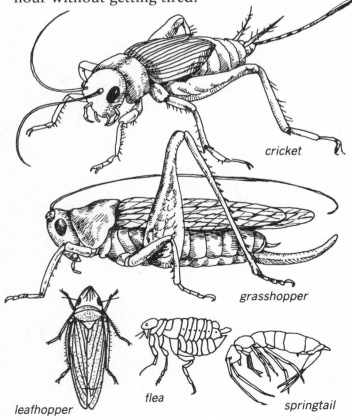

cricket

grasshopper

leafhopper

flea

springtail

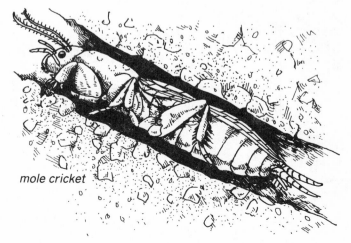

mole cricket

Flying

No matter how hard you flap, you'll never fly. You'll need a plane ticket to do that. And not all insects can fly either—only those with wings. Some, like house flies, have only two wings, but dragonflies, bees and butterflies have four wings each. How they use their wings differs too. Dragonflies raise their front pair of wings, while lowering their hind wings. Bees and butterflies, though, join the two wings on each side together to act as one big wing. Then they flap all four wings up and down at the same time. Some moths are such talented fliers that they can twist and turn in mid-air hundreds of times in a minute to avoid enemies.

Hovering

Like helicopters, many insects can hover. To do this they beat their wings rapidly. Dragonflies, sphinx moths and bee flies can all hover, but the real champs are the hover flies. They can hover in one place for hours.

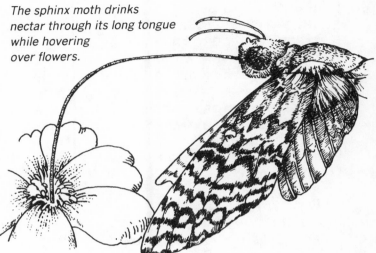

The sphinx moth drinks nectar through its long tongue while hovering over flowers.

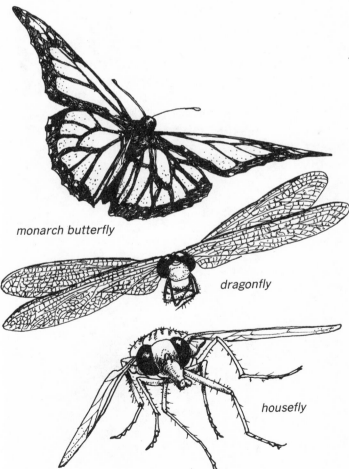

monarch butterfly

dragonfly

housefly

Move over, Arnold Schwarzenegger

Believe it or not, you and muscle-bound Arnold have the same number of muscles— 639. How many do you think a 5 or 6 cm (2 or 3 inch) long caterpillar has? More than 4000! It needs lots of muscles just to help it crawl around.

45

A clean sweep

What do you see when you look at an abandoned field, unmown ditch or wild meadow? Probably a lot of tall grass and wild flowers. But it's what you don't see that's so interesting. A casual walk into the grass usually sends dozens of creatures flipping, flopping, flying and hopping in every direction. How can you get a closer look at these insects? What you need is a sweep net. You can gently catch easy-to-see and hidden insects in your net, have a good look at them and then let them go.

You'll need:
a coat hanger
wire cutters
scissors
an old, light-coloured pillowcase with a
    hem around the top
a needle and thread (optional)
a pocket knife
an old broom handle or hockey stick
    shaft
some strong, bendable wire

1. Bend the hanger into a circle. Unravel the twisted end. Ask an adult to cut off the hook with the wire cutters.

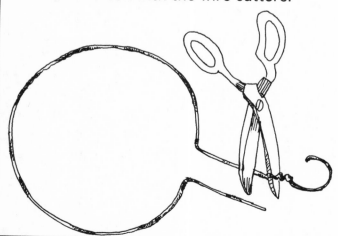

2. Cut a small opening in the hem of your pillowcase and thread your coat hanger through so that both ends stick out of the hole. The pillowcase seams should be on the inside of your net.

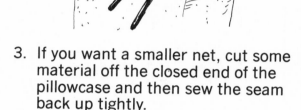

3. If you want a smaller net, cut some material off the closed end of the pillowcase and then sew the seam back up tightly.
4. Ask an adult to cut a deep notch, long enough for the wire ends of your hanger, on each side of the end of your broom handle.
5. Fit the hanger ends into the notches. Wrap some bendable wire tightly around the notches so that the net is held securely to the handle.

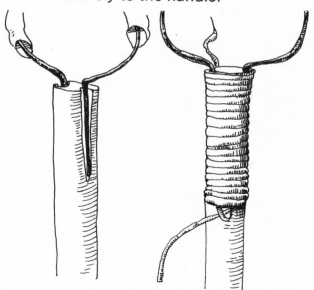

6. Drag your net back and forth through tall grass, wild flowers and low shrubs. Check your sweep net for some of these wonders. Remember — some insects will bite or sting in defence, so handle with care.

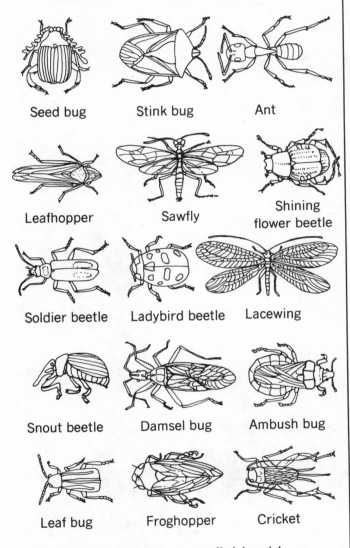

Seed bug   Stink bug   Ant

Leafhopper   Sawfly   Shining flower beetle

Soldier beetle   Ladybird beetle   Lacewing

Snout beetle   Damsel bug   Ambush bug

Leaf bug   Froghopper   Cricket

Others to look up in your field guide include treehoppers, mantids, grasshoppers, katydids, various caterpillars, aphids, shield-backed bugs and negro bugs.

I got one!

When you catch something in your net, you can get a closer look at it by carefully transferring it with tweezers into a container. Use a small, clear bottle, like a pill bottle, if the insect is small, or a large jam jar if it is big. Make sure there are air holes in the lids of your containers. To keep insects in your net from escaping while you are looking at something, simply fold the hanging part of your net up over the open end. When you've finished looking at your temporary treasures, carefully return them to where they were found.

Some Insects Up Close

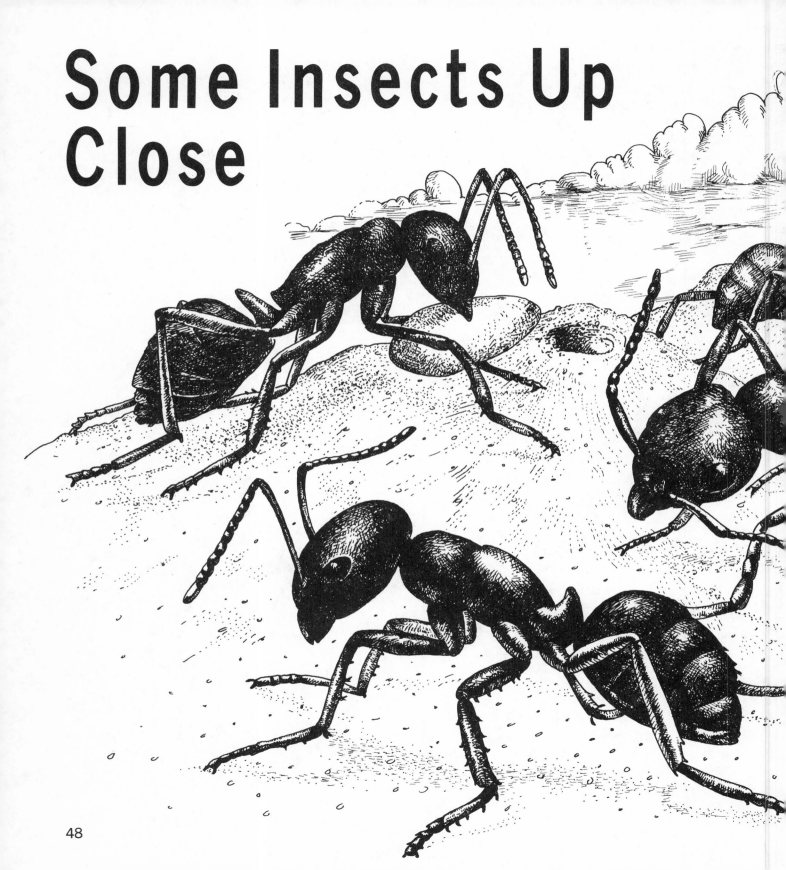

Have you ever seen an ant disappear into its tiny hole in the ground and tried to imagine where it was going, or watched a crawling caterpillar and wondered what it would turn into? Here's your chance to solve some of these insect mysteries. Step into the lives of a few of our most common but amazing insects. Discover how caterpillars turn into butterflies, what ants do underground, why only female mosquitoes bite, and much more.

Raising a monarch butterfly

When you were born, you looked like a very small version of the person you are today. But most insects start out life looking completely different from their adult form. Monarch butterflies, for example, go through four different stages during their metamorphosis (met-a-more-foe-sis), or period of "growing up." These are the egg, larva, pupa and adult stages. You can raise your own monarch butterfly and watch the whole process, from egg or caterpillar to adult in a little over a month. Monarch butterflies are easy to raise and beautiful to watch.

You'll need:
monarch butterfly eggs or caterpillars
   (2 or 3)
fresh milkweed plants daily
a small container of water
a large clear jar (1 L [1 quart] or more)
a long stick
cheesecloth or fine screening
an elastic

1. Pick part of a milkweed plant that has monarch eggs or caterpillars on it. Bring the plant and insect home and put the milkweed stem in a container of cool water to keep it from wilting. Extra milkweed leaves can be brought home at the same time and stored in water in the fridge for two to three days. This saves you a daily trip to the milkweed patch for caterpillar food.

2. Place a stick in the jar for the caterpillars to crawl on. Cover the jar's opening with cheesecloth or fine screening and secure it with an elastic. You must supply fresh milkweed leaves daily for your caterpillars to eat.

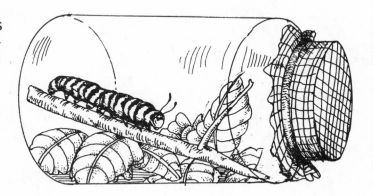

3. Take notes and/or photographs of the various stages in your butterfly's life. They will help you remember the experience and share it with others.
4. When the adult monarch butterfly has emerged, let it go free so that it may carry on with its life. If possible, it should be released where the original eggs or caterpillars were found.

How to find monarch eggs and caterpillars
June and early July are the best times to search for monarch eggs or caterpillars. Visit open fields or roadsides to find milkweed plants. Their large, pinkish blossoms smell beautiful and are easy to spot. Check under the milkweed's leaves for the tiny bun-shaped eggs. Or you may find the yellow, white and black striped caterpillars climbing on the stems or leaves. The bigger the caterpillar, the sooner it will turn into a chrysalis.

What you'll see:

Week 1:
Monarch butterfly eggs hatch in four to five days, producing a tiny yellow, black and white striped caterpillar. This is the monarch's larva stage. The caterpillar eats constantly and grows rapidly. As it grows, it sheds its skin to make more room.

Week 2:
At age two weeks your caterpillar is 2700 times its original size! Imagine what would happen if you grew that much? Watch out, Jolly Green Giant!

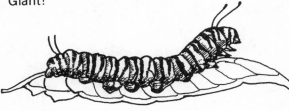

Week 3:
The caterpillar spins a silk pad on a leaf or branch. It attaches itself to the pad and hangs upside down. The larva's striped skin will gradually change into the emerald green case of the pupa, called a chrysalis. Inside this case the adult starts to form.

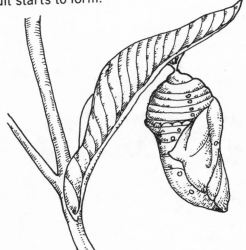

Week 4:
Within nine or ten days, the green coloured chrysalis fades, leaving a see-through pupal case. Through this "window" you will spy the bright orange and black folded wings of the adult, almost ready to come out.

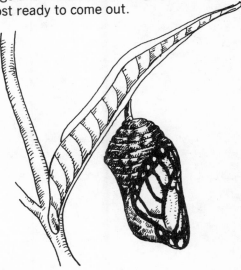

Week 5:
About two weeks after the chrysalis is formed, the adult butterfly splits it open and climbs out head first.

51

How to tell a butterfly from a moth

Butterflies and moths are closely related, like first cousins. Many people have trouble telling them apart, but once you know what to look for, it's easy to tell which is which.

When resting, butterflies close their wings high above their backs, but can't fold them. Moths fold their wings down on top of their backs at rest.

Butterflies have skinny antennae with knobs on the ends.
Many moths have feather-like antennae, or thread-like antennae without knobs.

Butterflies usually have long, slender bodies.
Moths have fat, often fuzzy bodies.

You won't see butterflies flying around at night or many moths during the day.

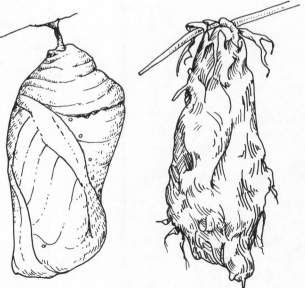

The third life stage (pupal stage) of a butterfly is a smooth chrysalis. A moth spends its pupal stage in a cocoon spun with silk.

Have a moth ball

You don't have to dress up like a moth to attract one. In fact, with a few simple materials you can host a party for moths, and other insects, and get a good look at some of your surprising neighbours. You may want to use a field guide to help identify some of your guests.

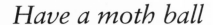

Sugaring

Just like kids, many insects love sweet stuff. You can attract moths and other insects by setting out a sweet and sticky treat. Moths are more easily attracted at dusk, but you can use the same bait and method for attracting other insects during the day.

You'll need:
sugar or molasses
stale fruit juice
spoiled, mashed up fruit (bananas work well)
a bowl and spoon
trees
an old paintbrush
a flashlight

1. Mix up the sugar, juice and fruit in a bowl.
2. Late in the day choose a tree, or trees, and use an old paintbrush to paint the mixture on the trunk.
3. Return about an hour later in the dark. Use your flashlight to see who's dropped in.
4. You can make a moth trail by painting several trees along a route that can be walked in 20-30 minutes. Try to end up where you started. By the time the last tree has been painted, some insects may already be at the first tree. Follow the route around, checking to see what has been attracted at each stop.

Light lovers

Have you ever noticed all the insects flying around street lights at night? Lights are often used to attract insects that fly in the evening, especially moths. Areas with lots of trees and flowers—like backyards, parks or woods—are good places to watch night fliers.

You'll need:

tacks

an old white sheet

a light (porch light, large flashlight or lantern)

a large glass jar and lid with holes punched in

a plant stem or twig to put inside the jar

1. Tack the sheet on the side of a building or from the branch of a tree.
2. Shine a bright light on the sheet at night.
3. You can stand very close to the sheet without scaring off the insects. When an insect lands on the sheet, try to catch it in your jar for a closer look. Let it go when you are finished.

Amazing ants

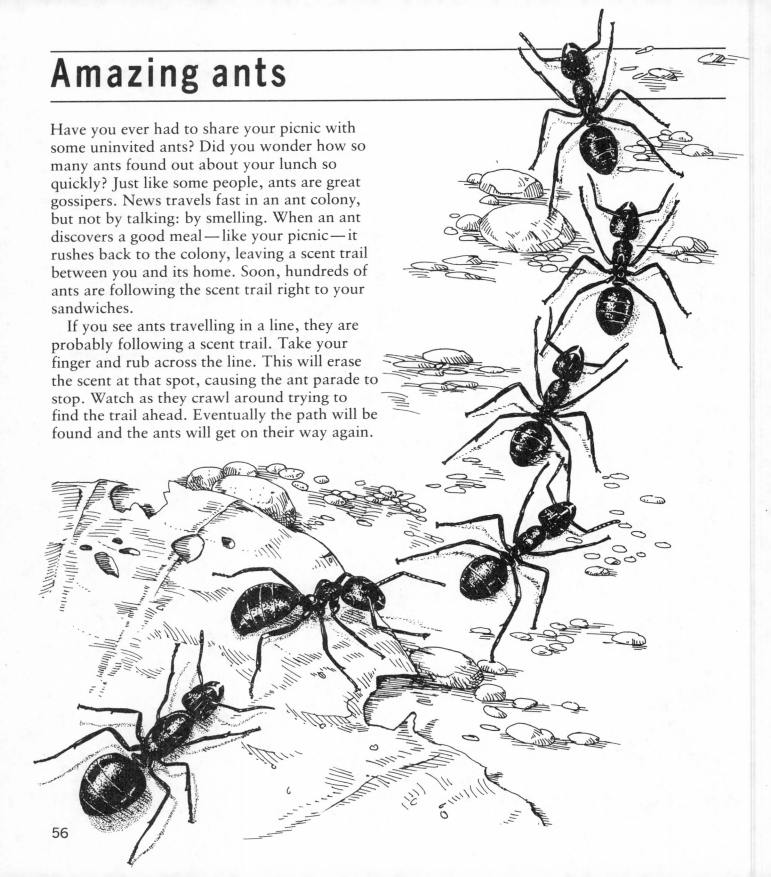

Have you ever had to share your picnic with some uninvited ants? Did you wonder how so many ants found out about your lunch so quickly? Just like some people, ants are great gossipers. News travels fast in an ant colony, but not by talking: by smelling. When an ant discovers a good meal—like your picnic—it rushes back to the colony, leaving a scent trail between you and its home. Soon, hundreds of ants are following the scent trail right to your sandwiches.

If you see ants travelling in a line, they are probably following a scent trail. Take your finger and rub across the line. This will erase the scent at that spot, causing the ant parade to stop. Watch as they crawl around trying to find the trail ahead. Eventually the path will be found and the ants will get on their way again.

An ant's life

Your community is full of people who live and work together. Ants also live in a type of community called a colony. Ants, like bees and termites, are called social insects. Different members of the colony have different roles and each role is critical to the success of the whole colony. Ants are divided into queens, males and workers. There is usually one queen for each colony and often thousands of workers. The queen rules the roost and lays all the eggs while the workers do all the chores.

Every fall a group of winged ants are produced who leave the nest to mate. If you see ants with wings, especially in a swarm, you know that these are the new queens and males. The males die as soon as mating is over. Each queen chooses a site for a new home, pulls off its wings and starts to burrow. Later she will lay thousands of eggs to start off the new colony.

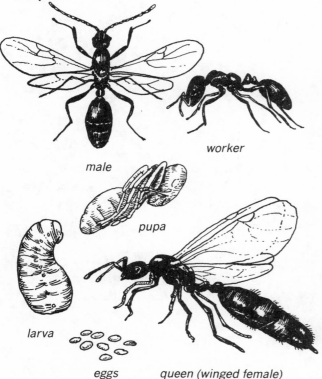

male

worker

pupa

larva

eggs

queen (winged female)

ANTennae

Since ants have poor eyesight, they use their antennae to help them find their way around. Each antenna has a sort of elbow in the middle, letting it bend and move around. The antennae are used for feeling, smelling, picking up vibrations and even taking the temperature. With all this use, the antennae need a lot of cleaning. In fact, ants are some of the fussiest and cleanest insects known. On the middle joint of each front leg is a little "comb" used for cleaning their bodies and especially their antennae. After the grooming is over, the ant uses its mouth to clean out the combs.

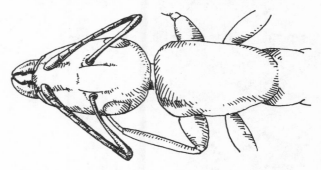

Did you know that . . .

- ☐ *there are more ants than any other creature on earth?*
- ☐ *ants are found everywhere on land except the polar regions?*
- ☐ *ants can lift up to 50 times their own weight? That's like you lifting two small cars at the same time.*
- ☐ *ants live an average of eight years? That's longer than any other insect.*

Ants are . . .

Carpenters

Carpenter ants live in wood, chewing tunnels through it. Why bother with all that work? The wood provides shelter, protection from predators and a place to nest. The carpenter ants don't eat wood; they feed on seeds, plant juices and other insects. Although these woodworkers usually live in dead logs and tree stumps, they sometimes invade people's homes and can cause a lot of damage to the structure.

Gardeners

Leaf-cutter ants have a clever way of "growing" their own food. They cut and carry pieces of leaves into their nests and "plant" them in special rooms. A type of fungus grows on the leaves and the ants eat the fungus.

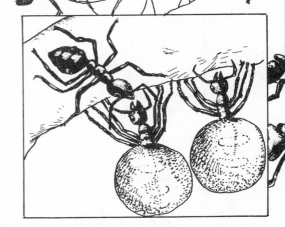

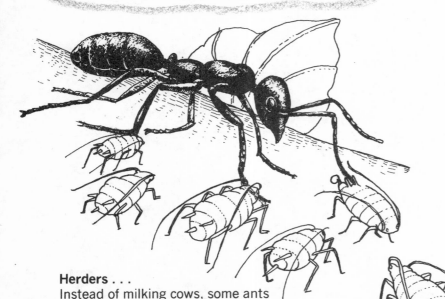

Herders . . .

Instead of milking cows, some ants "milk" aphids. An ant strokes the back of an aphid until the aphid secretes a tiny drop of "honeydew" from its abdomen. This sweet droplet is quickly licked up by the ant farmer. Ants are known to protect "herds" of aphids from predators in order to "milk" them for honeydew.

. . . and hoarders

Honey-pot ants like sweet drops, but theirs come from plants, not aphids. Since they live in the desert, their food is not always available. So when the plant sap is flowing, the workers collect large quantities to be stored for later. Where do they hoard it? Believe it or not, it's stored in the bodies of special ants that do nothing but hang from the ceiling of a room in the nest. These honey-pot ants are fed until their abdomens are so bloated, they can't move. They're like living refrigerators. When the other ants want some food, they visit the hanging honey-pots and make them regurgitate some of their sweet liquid.

58

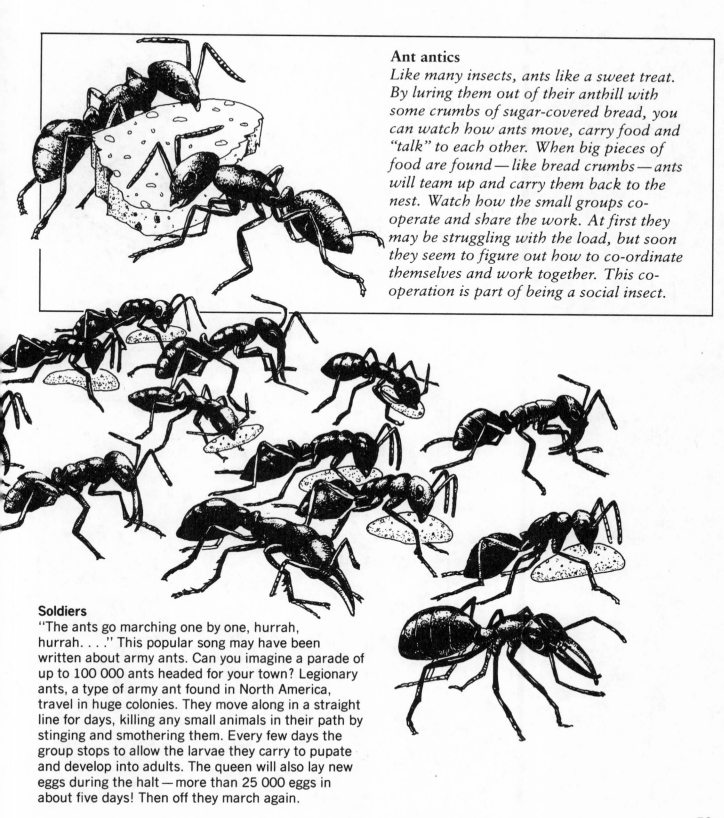

Ant antics

Like many insects, ants like a sweet treat. By luring them out of their anthill with some crumbs of sugar-covered bread, you can watch how ants move, carry food and "talk" to each other. When big pieces of food are found—like bread crumbs—ants will team up and carry them back to the nest. Watch how the small groups co-operate and share the work. At first they may be struggling with the load, but soon they seem to figure out how to co-ordinate themselves and work together. This co-operation is part of being a social insect.

Soldiers

"The ants go marching one by one, hurrah, hurrah. . . ." This popular song may have been written about army ants. Can you imagine a parade of up to 100 000 ants headed for your town? Legionary ants, a type of army ant found in North America, travel in huge colonies. They move along in a straight line for days, killing any small animals in their path by stinging and smothering them. Every few days the group stops to allow the larvae they carry to pupate and develop into adults. The queen will also lay new eggs during the halt—more than 25 000 eggs in about five days! Then off they march again.

An ant palace

If you could shrink down to ant-size and follow an ant into its home, you'd find a palace below the ground. The palace is ruled by a queen ant who is surrounded by thousands of servants (workers). Ant homes have lots of different rooms for eggs, larvae and pupae, pantries for food and even special rooms for their garbage. You can set up a mini-ant palace in your own home and see for yourself what goes on underground.

You'll need:
a large glass jar
soft, garden soil
a trowel
cheesecloth
an elastic band
tape
black paper
food for ants — sugar, honey, bread
   crumbs

1. Fill your jar with loosely packed soil, leaving 5 or 6 cm (2 or 3 inches) of space at the top.
2. Look for a colony of small black or brown ants in an open area like a roadside, backyard, driveway or sidewalk crack. Dig the ants up with your trowel. Try to find the biggest ant, the queen, and put her in your jar along with as many workers as you can get.

3. Secure the cheesecloth over the top of the jar with the elastic band.
4. Tape a piece of black paper around your jar up to the level of the earth.
5. To feed your ants, just sprinkle a little bit of sugar, honey and bread crumbs on top of the earth daily.
6. The ants will make a new colony and dig tunnels through the earth. The black paper encourages ants to dig right next to the glass. Remove the black paper for a short time every few days or so and peek in.
7. When you've finished watching your ant palace, return the ants to where you found them.

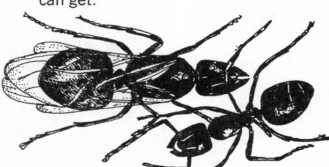

Amazing ant stories

☐ *Had an ant bath lately? Birds often let ants crawl all over them to help get them clean. The ants produce a chemical that kills lice and other tiny pests that live on birds.*

☐ *If you climb trees, keep a look out for ants. Dr. Edward O. Wilson found 43 species of ants on one tree in the Peruvian rain forest!*

☐ *Ever seen ants carrying a dead ant and wondered what they're doing? The corpses of ants give off special identifying odours that help workers know if the dead ant was a member of their colony. If it was, the pall-bearing ants carry their dead buddy off to the ant morgue — a special area that's like a compost heap.*

☐ *Ants communicate by using smells instead of sounds. Their bodies contain many different chemicals, each with its own odour and meaning. In their jaws, ants carry a chemical that signals an alarm, or call to war. If an ant's head is crushed accidentally, say by a person stepping on it, the alarm chemical is released and all the ants nearby get the message that a war has been declared. Ant soldiers will suddenly appear, ready to fight.*

☐ *Ants are smart. How do we know? A researcher built special mazes for testing some ants. The ants had to find their way from their nest to a dish of food by travelling through the maze of corridors. After doing it once, the ants simply followed their scent trail. But even when the scent trail was removed, the ants could still get through the maze, proving that they memorized the correct path.*

Beetlemania

What would you call a beetle that spends its day roaming around and around in a jar of flour? A confused flour beetle, of course! How do you think the ant-like stone beetle, death-watch beetle and handsome fungus beetle got their names?

There are more beetles than any other group of insects, and they range in size from almost invisible to as big as a man's hand. Despite the huge variety, you can look for a few simple features to help you recognize one of the gang. Beetles fly with only one pair of wings—the hind wings. When flying, the hard front wings lift out of the way and are carried high over the beetle's back. Another thing to look for is the mouth parts. All beetles are biters and chewers; some are serious crop pests, while others are superb natural pest controllers.

If you were a reporter, you could spend a lifetime on the "beetle beat." Here are a few "special features" to get you started.

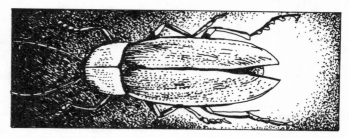

Light of love
What's as small as a jelly bean and glows in the dark? A lovesick firefly trying to find a mate. Wonder how they do it? Inside the firefly's abdomen are special organs that contain light-producing chemicals. When the male firefly is looking for a mate, it starts flashing. Different species flash at different times of the evening and also send different numbers of flashes at a time. A female only responds to the flashes of her own species.

Fireflies aren't the only light makers. Other insects that glow include some ground beetles, click beetles, midges, fungus gnats and springtails. In tropical areas, natives have been known to catch glowing insects to use like flashlights while travelling in dark jungles.

Bombardiers
What better way to escape enemies than to send up a smoke screen? The bombardier beetle does just that. Inside its abdomen, a bombardier has special chemical liquids that, when mixed together, explode out of its body. The result is a hot, smelly, smoky gas. As the chemicals explode, a series of pops goes off, like firecrackers, to scare the intruder. If that isn't enough, the hot gas will irritate the enemy's eyes and the smoke helps the beetle escape without being seen. Luckily for us, the gas bombs are dangerous to only very small enemies like other insects.

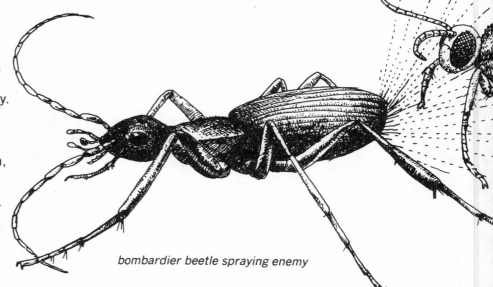

bombardier beetle spraying enemy

Ladybug, ladybug fly away home . . .

Have you ever tried to tell a ladybug's age by counting its spots? Well, you might as well give up. The number of spots tells the kind of ladybug it is, not its age. There are more than 5000 different kinds of ladybugs. Most of them are terrific insect pest controllers, eating thousands of aphids, white flies and other plant eaters.

Undertakers

Burying beetles are the undertakers of the insect world. When they come across the dead body of a small animal in the woods, they set to work. By digging big holes underneath the animal, the body eventually sinks down below ground level and is covered over. Burying beetles don't do this to tidy up —the females lay their eggs nearby and the larvae feed on the corpse.

Make a living lantern

Light up the night with this living lantern. Batteries not included.

You'll need:
a hammer
a nail
a jam jar with a lid
fireflies

1. Hammer the nail through the jar lid to make several air holes.
2. At dusk, take your jar and lid out to a field where you've seen fireflies.
3. Carefully catch three or four fireflies in your hands, place them in your jar and put the lid on. You'll have to be quick, since fireflies are fast fliers.
4. The fireflies in your jar will continue to produce their light flashes for about an hour. You can use your jar as a living lantern to go for a walk in the dark. Release the fireflies where you found them.

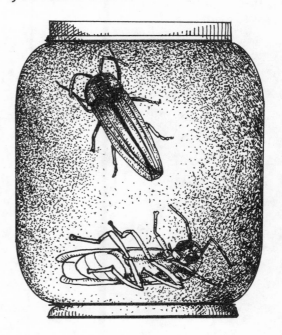

Industrious insects

What do silk scarves, shellac, honey, make-up and furniture polish have in common? They're all made from insect products. Besides providing these useful materials for people, insects help us in many different ways.

Farmers' friends
If you like plump peaches and crunchy cucumbers, some of your best friends are insects. Without the pollinating activities of thousands of insects, especially honey bees, there wouldn't be as many flowers and trees or fruits and vegetables. In fact, many farmers raise bees especially to help pollinate their orchards and other crops. How does it work? When a bee visits a flower for a drink of nectar, its hairy body picks up grains of pollen and carries them to the next flower. Here the pollen brushes off against the flower's pistil and pollinates the flower so it can produce fruits and seeds.

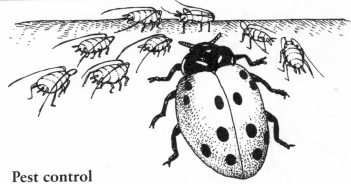

Pest control
You've heard of fighting fire with fire, but what about fighting insects with insects? Scientists use some insects to wipe out others that are harming crops. This "biological control" can be just as efficient as chemical sprays.

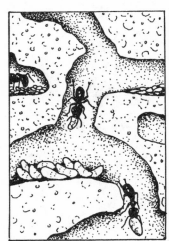

Soil making
You use a shovel to turn the soil in your garden, but ants do the same thing using only their bodies—they are amazing soil mixers. Other insects help to break down dead plant and animal remains into compost for the soil. All this composting and soil mixing give plants more food and make it easier for plant roots to grow through the earth.

Insect scientists

Just like people, thousands of insects go to work every day in laboratories and research centres worldwide. Insects are commonly used in scientific research to study genetics, evolution and even pollution. They make great guests in the laboratory since they're easy to raise and feed, they produce lots of young and many have short life cycles.

Insect surgeons?

☐ *Maggots of various blow flies were used to clean the wounds of soldiers in the past. A substance called allantoin in the insects' wastes actually fought infection and saved lives. Luckily, antibiotics have replaced the use of maggots today.*

☐ *Primitive people in some parts of the world today use insects such as ants and carabid beetles instead of stitches for closing wounds. These insects are enticed to bite a cut so that their strong jaws hold the two edges of the wound together. The insects' bodies are then cut off, leaving the heads to act as clamps. Once the cut heals, the insect heads are removed.*

A honey of a job

The next time you spread honey on your toast, remember this. Honey bees must visit between 60 000 and 90 000 flower tubes to collect enough nectar to make a thimbleful of honey. In spite of this hard work, a single hive may make up to a kilogram (two pounds) of honey per day—those are busy bees!

If you suck on the base of a clover flower you can taste the sweetness of nectar. But how does a bee change nectar into honey? First, a bee visits enough flowers to fill up the stomach-like honey sac inside its body. When it returns to the hive, the bee spits up the nectar onto the mouth parts of other bees. They pass the nectar back and forth over their tongues, allowing some of the water to evaporate. The nectar is mixed with saliva and stored in open cells in the comb. Here it loses more water and eventually thickens into honey. The bees now seal the honey in the wax storage cells and save it for later. With a hive full of honey, the bees can stay warm and well fed in their home all winter long.

Biters and stingers

When it comes to biting and stinging insects, it's a matter of "heads or tails." Some use their mouths to pierce your skin, while others use the opposite end. Whatever way they do it, it's usually the females who do the "dirty work." Here's why.

Mini-vampires

If you've been stabbed and jabbed by blood-sucking insects then you know how annoying, and sometimes painful, these mini-vampires can be. The needle-like mouth parts of insects like mosquitoes don't actually bite you—they pierce your skin. The female mosquito spits saliva into the wound to stop your blood from clotting and then she fills her "tank" with blood before flying off. Why are the females so bloodthirsty? Your blood is essential for the production of eggs in the female's body. So, like it or not, every bite may mean hundreds more mosquitoes to come.

Other flying blood-suckers to avoid include black flies, no-see-ums, deer flies and stable flies. Besides being irritating, some biters also carry diseases that they can pass on to people through their saliva.

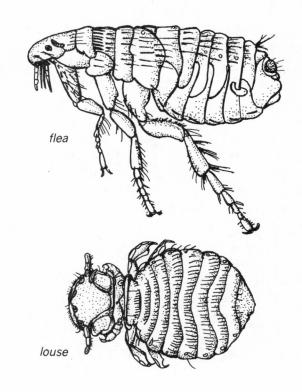
flea

louse

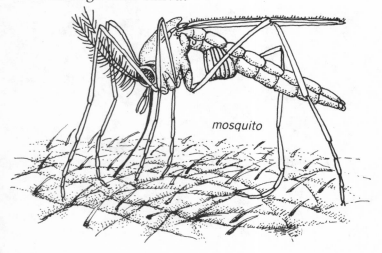
mosquito

Body bugs

Just thinking about fleas and lice can get you scratching. Fleas are wingless, hopping insects found in the hairs and feathers of many pets. And they're nearly impossible to catch—they jump 200 times their own body length in one bound. You're left scratching your head in frustration, and your pet is still scratching too! Occasionally, pets' fleas will bite people, but they won't hang around since you don't taste good to them.

Lice are not nice. Two kinds—pubic lice and body and head lice—can attack people, sucking blood and causing itching and discomfort. These lice, sometimes called "cooties," are tiny, flat insects that cling to your hair with their strong, curved claws.

Mind your own beeswax

When a bee stings, it's telling you to stay away, or mind your own beeswax. You are seen as a threat to the bee or the hive, and stinging is its best defence. Only female bees, wasps and some ants sting since the stinger is really the insect's ovipositor — the tube for laying eggs. Males don't have them. You may have heard that once a bee stings, it dies. This is true only for a honey bee. Its stinger has tiny barbs on it that get stuck in your skin. When the honey bee tries to pull the stinger out, its abdomen usually rips off and the bee dies. Other bees and wasps have smooth stingers that can go in and out like a needle, stinging many times. When you're stung, the insect injects poison from little glands in its abdomen. It's the poison that causes the irritation and swelling. Some people are highly allergic to bee stings and must see a doctor immediately.

Fighting back

Spraying and smearing insect repellents on your skin is one way of avoiding annoying bugs. Here are some others:

- ☐ *Wear long sleeves, long pants, hat and neck scarf.*
- ☐ *Buy or make a bug hat for really bad days (see page 31).*
- ☐ *Dress in light colours. Dark clothing seems to attract mosquitoes.*
- ☐ *Sit around a fire at night. Mosquitoes usually avoid smoke.*

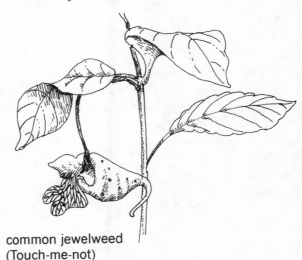

common jewelweed
(Touch-me-not)

Once bitten (or stung) . . .

If you've been bitten or stung, try one of these "home remedies" to relieve the pain or itching.

- ☐ *Jewelweed is a great anti-itching plant that grows in wet areas — right where the mosquitoes breed. Just break open a stem and rub the clear juice on your mosquito bite. The itching will stop almost instantly.*

- ☐ *A paste made from baking soda and water can be spread on stings or bites to relieve pain and control swelling.*

Insect Survival

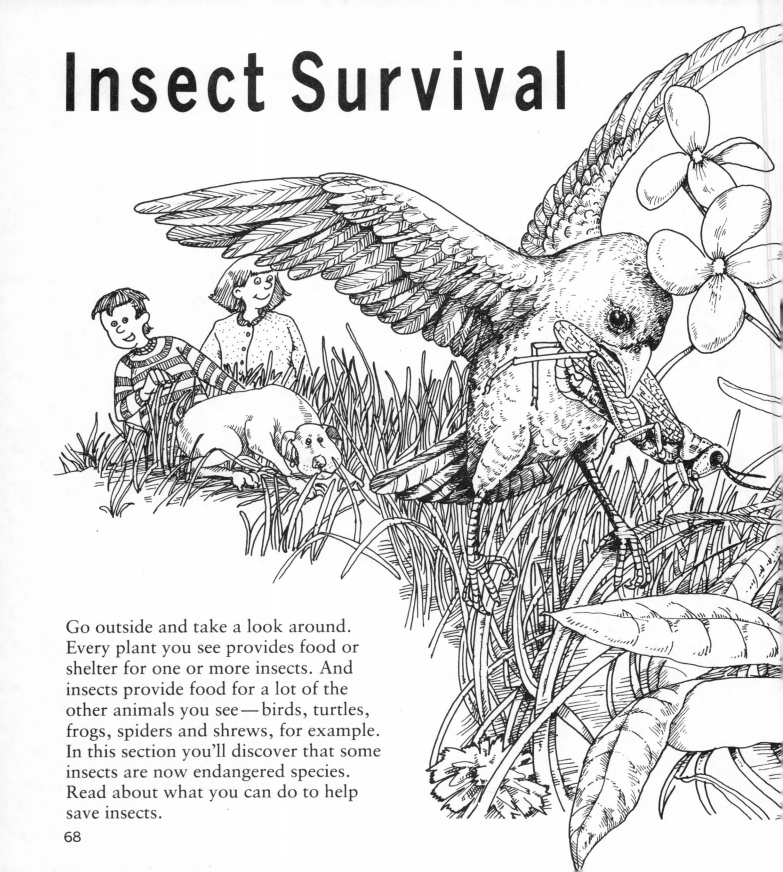

Go outside and take a look around. Every plant you see provides food or shelter for one or more insects. And insects provide food for a lot of the other animals you see—birds, turtles, frogs, spiders and shrews, for example. In this section you'll discover that some insects are now endangered species. Read about what you can do to help save insects.

Plant-eating insects

Think of a plant. Chances are it's probably eaten by one or more insects. From the scale insect, that's smaller than a raisin, to the walking stick, that's longer than a watermelon, insects inhabit and eat their way through a huge variety of plants. And no part of a plant is left untouched. Roots, stems, leaves, buds, flowers, bark, cones, fruits and seeds are all insect food. A single tree may be home to several thousand insects.

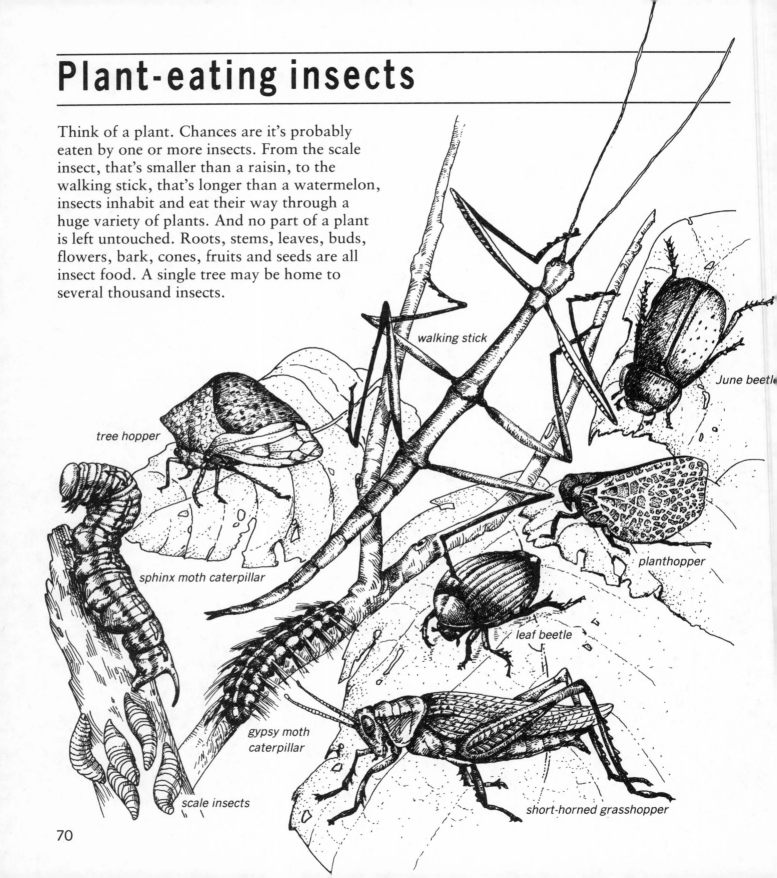

walking stick

June beetle

tree hopper

planthopper

sphinx moth caterpillar

leaf beetle

gypsy moth caterpillar

scale insects

short-horned grasshopper

Suckers and chewers

How about using a straw to eat your meal? Some insects, like aphids and plant hoppers, make tiny holes in plant stems and suck out the juices with their straw-like mouth parts. Beetles, caterpillars and other insects with chewing mouth parts actually eat pieces of plants. If large numbers of plant eaters, like tent caterpillars or gypsy moth larvae, get together for a feast they can eat all of the leaves in hectares of forests.

Big eaters

When Colorado potato beetles find huge fields of potatoes, they sit down to an "all-you-can-eat" banquet. They don't stop munching until they run out of food. These insects can be real pests to farmers. How can they be stopped? Farmers spend millions of dollars each year spraying chemicals to control insect pests. But there is another way. Farmers could plant potatoes in many smaller fields instead of one big one. If other crops, such as beans, were planted in between, they would act like road blocks to the potato beetles. Although smaller fields of different crops are more difficult and expensive to look after, they might help reduce the billions of dollars lost to insect damage every year, without damaging the environment.

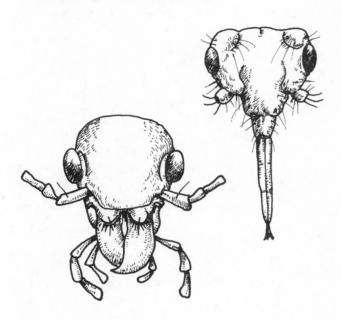

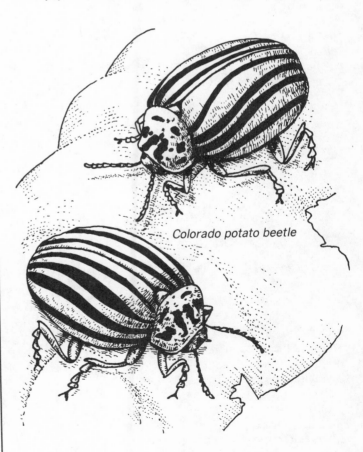

Colorado potato beetle

Mexican jumping beans

The amazing jumping and rolling of the seeds from various Mexican plants is not magic. It's caused by the movements of a moth larva eating the seed from the inside out.

Insect-eating plants

If you like science fiction, you've probably read about incredible flesh-eating plants that terrorize people and animals. But did you know that about 45 different kinds of meat-eating (carnivorous) plants really exist? They don't attack people, of course, but they do trap and digest a variety of tiny insects for food.

Trap doors

Bladderwort uses a tricky trapdoor to catch unsuspecting insects. It grows in the water of ponds and ditches and has pouch-like bladders that are attached to floating leaves. The bladders are fringed with hairs, so when an insect touches the hairs, a trapdoor swings open, the bladder inflates and the prey is sucked inside.

Clamming up

Venus fly traps are famous everywhere but actually only grow in North and South Carolina in the United States. Their hinged leaves are fringed with long bristles that are very sensitive to touch. When disturbed, the leaf snaps shut, like a clam, trapping its prey inside.

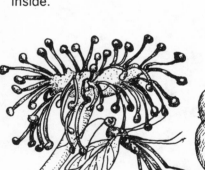

Sticky stuff

Sundews may be small, but they're tough on insects. This bog plant gets its name because of its leaves' long hairs, tipped with drops of sticky moisture. Insects get stuck to the glue-like substance on the hairs. Then the leaves fold over to enclose the insect in a sort of temporary stomach.

◁ In the drink

If you were an insect, you wouldn't want to stop for a drink from the pitcher plant. It attracts insects to its liquid-filled pitchers and then downward-pointing hairs prevent the insects from escaping. Once in the jug, the prey drowns and is soon digested.

Be a pitcher plant

You can catch an insect the same way a pitcher plant does, but instead of eating your catch, just have a close look at it before letting it go.

You'll need:
a plastic funnel
a sharp knife
a piece of juicy fruit or fruit juice
a wide-mouth jar

1. Ask an adult to cut off the narrow part of the funnel so that the opening is about 1 cm (½ inch) across.
2. Rub the piece of fruit over the inside of the funnel or pour some fruit juice on it so that the funnel is sticky and sweet smelling.
3. Place the fruit in the bottom of the jar.
4. Set the funnel in the mouth of the jar with the narrow part of the funnel pointing down.
5. Place your jar outside in an open area, like a field or backyard, and wait for your first visitor. Watch what happens when a fly or wasp lands on the funnel. The fruit will attract it down the funnel into the jar below, just as a pitcher plant attracts its prey. Once inside the jar, the insect will not be able to get out until you take the funnel away.

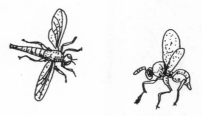

Born to eat

You use a knife, fork and cup for eating and drinking, but what do insects use? They have many special body parts adapted not only for eating their food, but also for catching and carrying it. Some of their eating equipment is similar to items you may have around the house.

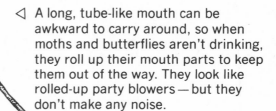

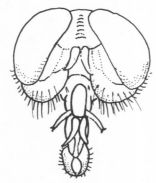

▷

You could say that a house fly has a sponge for a tongue. The wide, fleshy tip on its mouth parts absorbs liquids on contact. Flies must be great at cleaning up spills!

◁ A long, tube-like mouth can be awkward to carry around, so when moths and butterflies aren't drinking, they roll up their mouth parts to keep them out of the way. They look like rolled-up party blowers — but they don't make any noise.

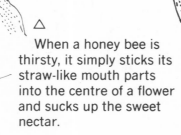

△

When a honey bee is thirsty, it simply sticks its straw-like mouth parts into the centre of a flower and sucks up the sweet nectar.

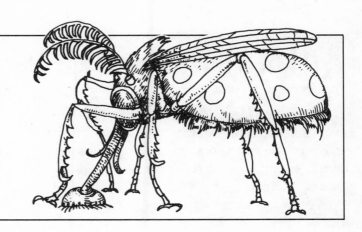

Incredible insects

Imagine that you could design your own insect. Choose from among the adaptations of the super eaters on this page, as well as from any ideas for getting around you've seen throughout the book, and create your own incredible insect. Give your creation a name. Here's an example of an imaginary insect. What would you call it?

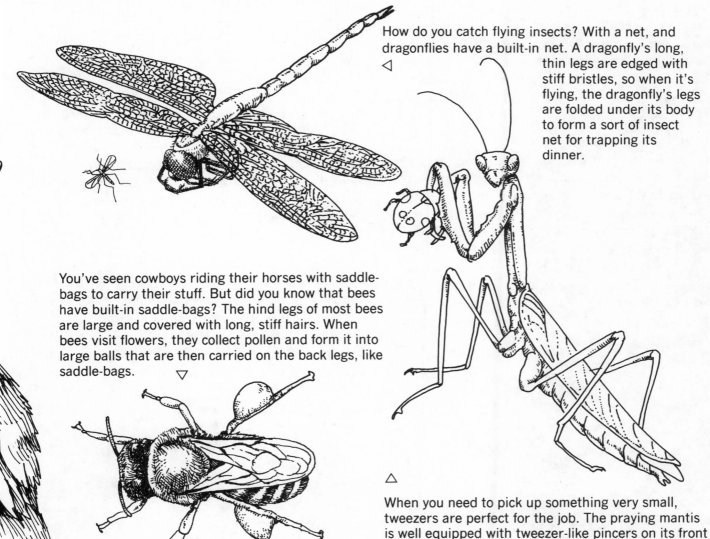

How do you catch flying insects? With a net, and dragonflies have a built-in net. A dragonfly's long, thin legs are edged with stiff bristles, so when it's flying, the dragonfly's legs are folded under its body to form a sort of insect net for trapping its dinner.

You've seen cowboys riding their horses with saddle-bags to carry their stuff. But did you know that bees have built-in saddle-bags? The hind legs of most bees are large and covered with long, stiff hairs. When bees visit flowers, they collect pollen and form it into large balls that are then carried on the back legs, like saddle-bags.

When you need to pick up something very small, tweezers are perfect for the job. The praying mantis is well equipped with tweezer-like pincers on its front legs. It can grab small insects and hold on tight until it eats them.

Animal insect eaters

In one year, one pair of pomace flies could produce enough new flies to reach from the earth to the sun. Luckily, there are lots of insect eaters around to help keep populations under control.

We owe our thanks mostly to birds and fish, but who else eats insects? Many thousands of animals depend on insects for survival, from frogs, snakes, lizards and turtles, to shrews, bats, mice, spiders and other insects too.

You know how hard it is to catch a fly, so how do animal insect eaters manage to get enough insects to survive? Take a look at these terrific insect trappers.

Stick out your tongue

How far can you stick out your tongue? If you were an ant-eater, the answer would be 38 cm (15 inches)! After ripping open an ant nest with its claws, the ant-eater sticks its tube-like snout into the hole. At the end of its nose is a small hole where the ant-eater sticks out its sticky, worm-like tongue. The ants stick to its tongue and the ant-eater slides its tongue back and swallows them.

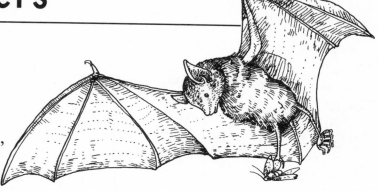

Hello . . . hello . . . hello . . .

Have you ever stood in a big empty room, called out and heard your echo? The echo is caused when sound from your call bounces off the room's walls and back to your ears, so you hear it again. Insect-eating bats use echoes to find their dinner. Their high-pitched squeaks bounce off flying insects and come back to the bats. Depending on where the echo comes from and how long it takes to hear, the bats can tell in what direction the insects are and how far away they are.

Monkeying around

Chimpanzees use tools to get at tasty termites. But they don't use monkey wrenches—just sticks. A chimp pokes a long stick into a termite's castle-like mud nest and digs out the insects. Then it licks off the termites clinging to the stick or eats them with its fingers.

Hungry as a bear

Winnie the Pooh sure loved honey. So do lots of bears. Instead of going to the honey jar, real bears find a honey bee hive, rip it open with their claws and scoop out the delicious honey inside, along with pawfuls of bees. What about all the bee stings? Bears don't seem to mind. Perhaps they figure "no pain, no gain."

Flying vacuums?

Imagine vacuuming up insects in mid-air. That's what Whip-poor-wills and nighthawks do. The short, weak beaks of these birds open wide as they fly, scooping insects right out of the air.

Edible insects

"Pass the ants, please." If you were invited to a fancy party, you might find insects on the hors d'oeuvres tray—chocolate-covered ants and bees, tinned grasshoppers or even fried agave grubs. Eating insects is nothing new, however. People in various countries have been munching on grubs, locusts, cicadas, crickets, caterpillars, termites, ants and large beetles and bugs for thousands of years. In fact, grubs are the only source of protein for many Australian aborigines. Tempted to taste a bug yourself? Check out a local specialty food shop and happy munching!

Insects in danger

How many people live in your town or city? If you live in a big city there may be more than a million people, or a small town may have only a few thousand. Now try to imagine the huge insect population. On average, there are about 200 000 insects for every one person on earth. Of course, just like small towns and big cities, the numbers are not evenly spread. In general, there are more insects in warm climates than in cold climates.

Even though there are lots of insects, some kinds are becoming endangered. Without help, these endangered insects may disappear from the earth forever. So what? Insects may not be everyone's favourite wildlife, but they are a vital part of the natural world and contribute a great deal to our way of life. They provide food for thousands of birds, mammals and fish, help pollinate flowers, fruits and vegetables and provide people with products such as honey and silk. Why are some insects becoming endangered?

Like many endangered species, some insects' biggest problem is the loss of habitat — a safe site for breeding, feeding and sheltering. Tropical rain forests, where more than half of all the world's insects live, are being destroyed. And wetland areas that are home to millions of insects are being drained. Insects are losing their homes!

For some insects their beauty is their worst enemy. Some of the most treasured collector's items are large and beautifully coloured butterflies and moths. Some collectors pay a lot of money for rare species. This only encourages people to look for them, kill and sell them. Unfortunately, the more endangered a species is, the more it is sought after.

Another problem for insects may be competition from new neighbours. Each country or part of a country has its own native species of plants and animals, including insects. Under natural conditions they all live together in a balanced ecosystem. But if you

Panaxia

Vanessa cardui

Papilio childrenae oedippus

introduce a new plant, animal or disease from a different country into an ecosystem, the balance may become upset. For example, starlings are the most abundant birds in North America today, but they've only been here since the late 19th century. An Englishman introduced the starling to North America because he wanted to have all the birds here that were mentioned in Shakespeare's plays. Unfortunately, many birds that were already here, such as the Eastern Bluebird, have suffered. Starlings outcompete bluebirds for nest holes and are partly to blame for a decline in the bluebird's population.

Save the insects!

Want to help, but don't know where to start? Here are some things you can do to save insects.

- ☐ Stop swatting and spraying every insect you see; learn how to live alongside them. Some insects, like mosquitoes, will always be pesty, but you needn't worry about ladybugs or praying mantids, so let them be.
- ☐ Concentrate on observing insects in nature, rather than collecting them.
- ☐ Support groups that are working to protect wildlife by volunteering time or donating money to help pay for research and habitat protection. You can raise money by doing anything from washing cars to selling popcorn. And your support does make a difference. In Santa Cruz, California, where a house-building company owned land on which monarch butterflies lived, the Xerces Society's Monarch Project worked with the company and the government to set aside part of the land. Now both humans and butterflies have homes.
- ☐ Introduce some friends to the fascinating world of insects. Start a bug club at school and help teach the rest of the students about the importance of protecting insects. The more people know, the more they'll care and want to help.

The BUG CLUB presents a Fundraiser to Help Save the Rain Forests

- ☐ Find out what is being done in other countries to help protect insect habitats. For instance, tropical rain forests are home to thousands of kinds of insects. If the rain forests are destroyed, we will lose much of the diversity of insect life. International environmental groups such as World Wildlife Fund are working to save tropical rain forests in Central and South America. They use donations to help buy up rain forests and protect them forever.

Hide and seek

If you wanted to hide in a forest, you'd wear greens and browns to blend in with the background. Many insects are specially coloured for hiding, too. Some are even shaped to help them hide better. Insects are disguised to look like sticks, leaves, needles, thorns, flowers, bark and even bird droppings! Why bother with these elaborate disguises? To avoid being eaten by birds.

Here's a chance to pretend you're a hungry bird. Can you find the 14 insects hiding in this picture? Turn to page 96 for the answers.

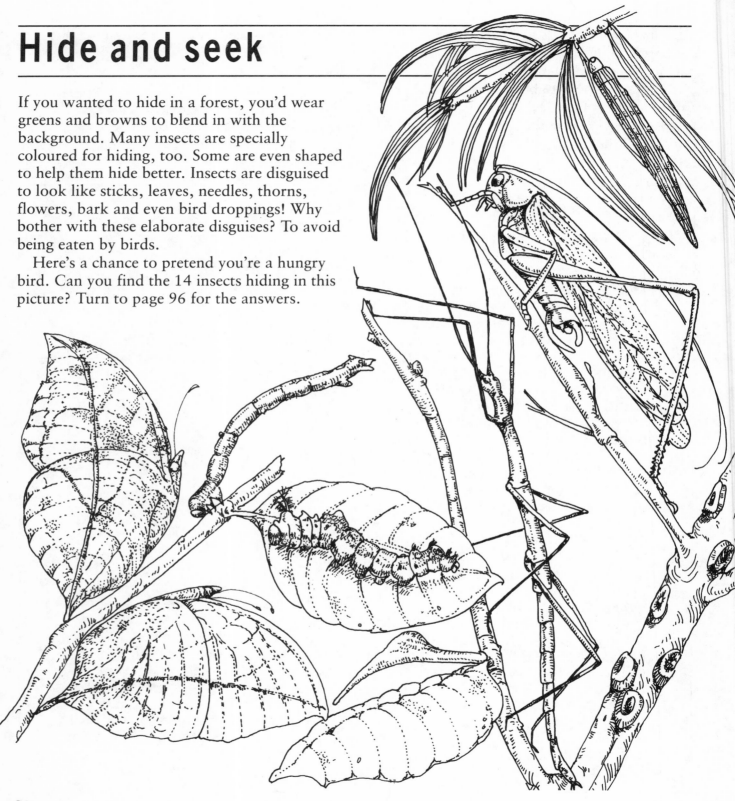

Insect Impostors

Some creatures look like insects, but they're not. They're impostors. Find out the difference between insects and such non-insects as spiders and centipedes. Discover how to get a spider to spin a web for you, and how to collect webs. If only Miss Muffet had known how neat spiders really are, she'd never have run away.

Who's an insect and who isn't?

Do all of the creatures on this page look like insects to you? Well, they're not. Some of them are insect impostors. How can you tell real insects from non-insects?

All adult insects share certain characteristics. (Immature insects are so different that there's no easy way to tell them — only practice.) All adult insects have:

- ☐ 6 legs
- ☐ 3 body parts: head, thorax, abdomen
- ☐ 2 antennae
- ☐ most have 1 or 2 pairs of wings

Now try guessing who's an insect and who's not. (Answers on page 96.)

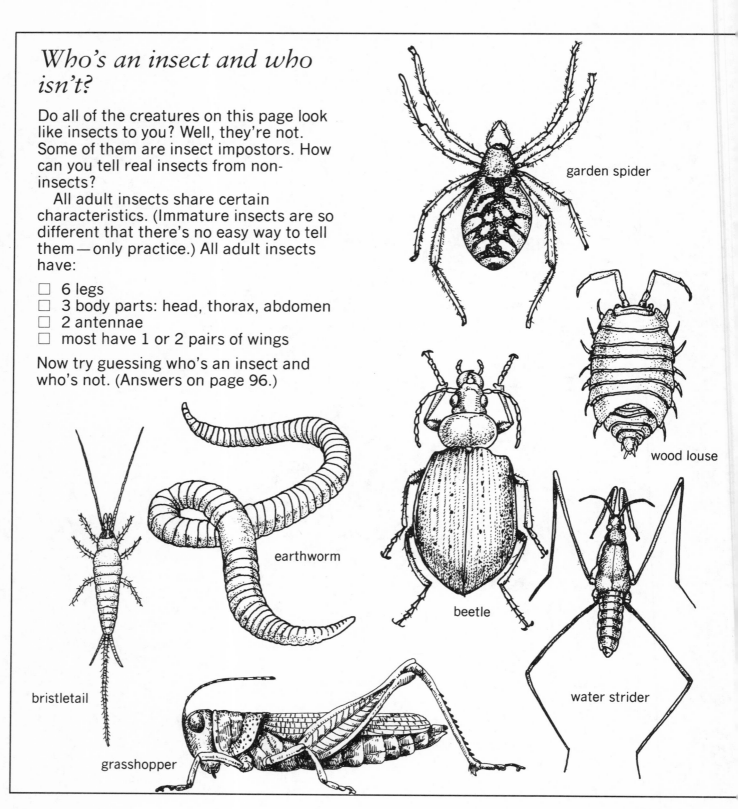

garden spider

wood louse

earthworm

beetle

water strider

bristletail

grasshopper

84

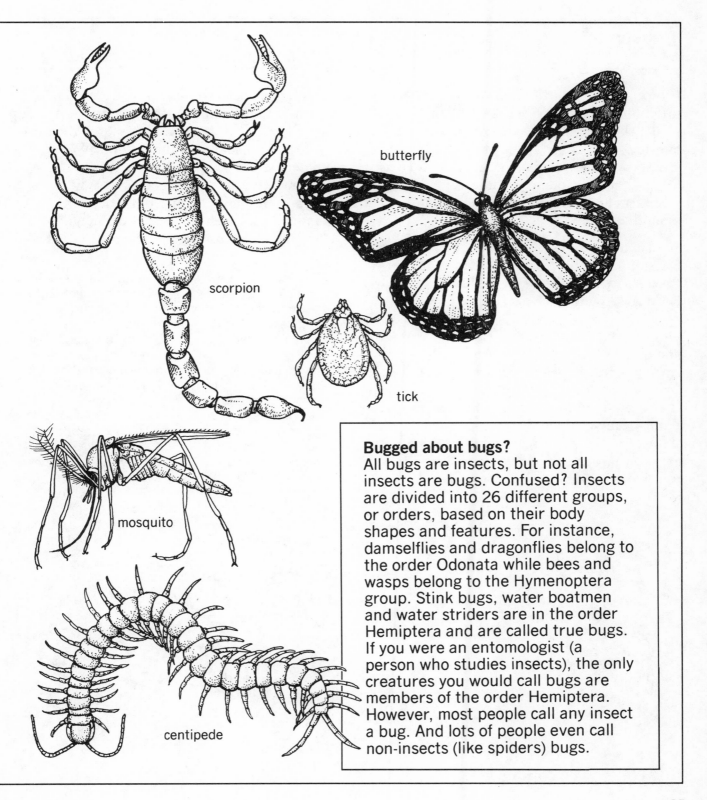

scorpion

butterfly

tick

mosquito

centipede

Bugged about bugs?
All bugs are insects, but not all insects are bugs. Confused? Insects are divided into 26 different groups, or orders, based on their body shapes and features. For instance, damselflies and dragonflies belong to the order Odonata while bees and wasps belong to the Hymenoptera group. Stink bugs, water boatmen and water striders are in the order Hemiptera and are called true bugs. If you were an entomologist (a person who studies insects), the only creatures you would call bugs are members of the order Hemiptera. However, most people call any insect a bug. And lots of people even call non-insects (like spiders) bugs.

Along came a spider . . .

It's too bad that Little Miss Muffet left her tuffet in such a hurry. If she had stayed a while, she would have been fascinated by the hunting skills of the visiting spider. Next time you see a spider, don't run. Sit and watch as it prepares to trap its supper of insects. Remember — spiders aren't insects, they're only insect look-alikes.

Silk spinners
Did you know that spider silk is said to be stronger than steel wire of the same size? Besides weaving silk into a strong, insect-catching web, spiders use silk to tie up their prey so it can't escape. Spiders also use silk for lining burrows and making egg cases and drag lines, like the line Miss Muffet's spider used to drop in on her.

The silk used in spinning comes from special glands, called spinnerets, in the spider's abdomen. It is actually liquid when it comes out, but hardens immediately into an amazingly stretchy and strong material.

Wanderers and web builders
Not all spiders spin webs to trap food. A group of spiders called the wanderers catch their prey by hunting, usually on the ground. Web builders and wanderers have different equipment to help them get food. When you find a spider, try to figure out whether it's a wanderer or a web builder. Use a magnifying glass and check for these features:

Wanderers
- Two large front eyes and six smaller eyes. Good eyesight enables them to watch for predators and prey.
- Large and powerful jaws are needed to grab and hold prey.
- Hair on the legs (and bodies) acts as sensors to help feel the way along the ground and find prey.
- Feet have two claws separated by a hairy pad to help grip on slippery surfaces.

Web builders
- Eight tiny eyes and poor eyesight. They use their sense of touch, instead, to feel vibrations on their web and locate prey.
- Smaller and weaker jaws; the web helps hold prey.
- Long, skinny legs allow better balance and quick, agile movements on the web.
- Feet have three claws; the middle claw hooks over the silken threads of the web.

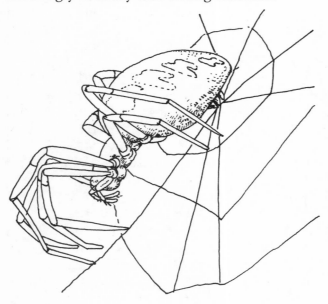

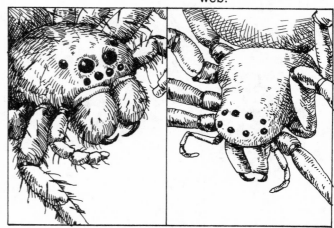

Up, up and away

Ballooning isn't just a sport for people, it's also a way of leaving home for some baby spiders. Young spiders climb to the tops of weed stalks or fence posts, point their abdomens in the air and release long threads of silk. The breeze catches the silk and gently lifts the spiderlings into the air, carrying them off like balloons. Some may travel hundreds of kilometres (miles)! You may see spiderlings floating by, especially in early fall.

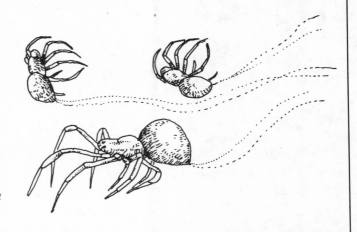

Sneaky spiders

If you were an insect, spiders would be your number one enemy. In fact, spiders are the most important insect catchers in the world. How do they do it? Some build clever traps, while others have bodies specially adapted for hunting. Here are a few of their amazing talents.

Jumping spiders can jump more than 50 times their own length to catch a meal. You'd have to leap the length of a football field to match that! They stalk their prey carefully and then jump into the air, landing right on top of the surprised insect.

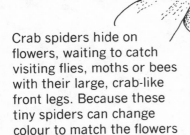

Crab spiders hide on flowers, waiting to catch visiting flies, moths or bees with their large, crab-like front legs. Because these tiny spiders can change colour to match the flowers on which they sit, they are very hard to see. Take a close look at some of the flowers in your garden and see if you can spot one of these well-disguised spiders.

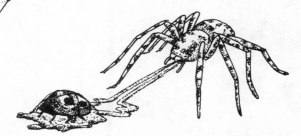

Spitting is considered rude, especially at the table, unless you're a spitting spider. It shoots a glue-like liquid from its fangs on to unlucky insects. The victims get stuck in their tracks and can't escape the hungry spider.

Step into my parlour . . .

When you go spider watching, you can see different kinds of spiders as well as the different traps they use to catch their prey. Spiders spin all kinds of different webs including cobwebs, sheet webs and funnel webs. Wanderers have some neat homes too. Take a look at some of these traps and how they're used to catch supper.

Cobweb
When you forget to dust in the corners of your bedroom, you might find that a spider has moved in. Cobwebs are common in houses. Spiders use them to trap house flies. ▷

Trapdoors △
Named for its tricky home, the trapdoor spider digs a tube-like trap underground, lined with silk. The tube is covered with a lid made of silk and soil, hinged with silk. It's sort of like a manhole cover with a hinge. The spider hides in its burrow with the trapdoor open just enough to peek out. As soon as an insect comes along, the spider jumps out, paralyzes it with a bite and then pulls it down inside the trap.

trapdoor spider catching a ladybug

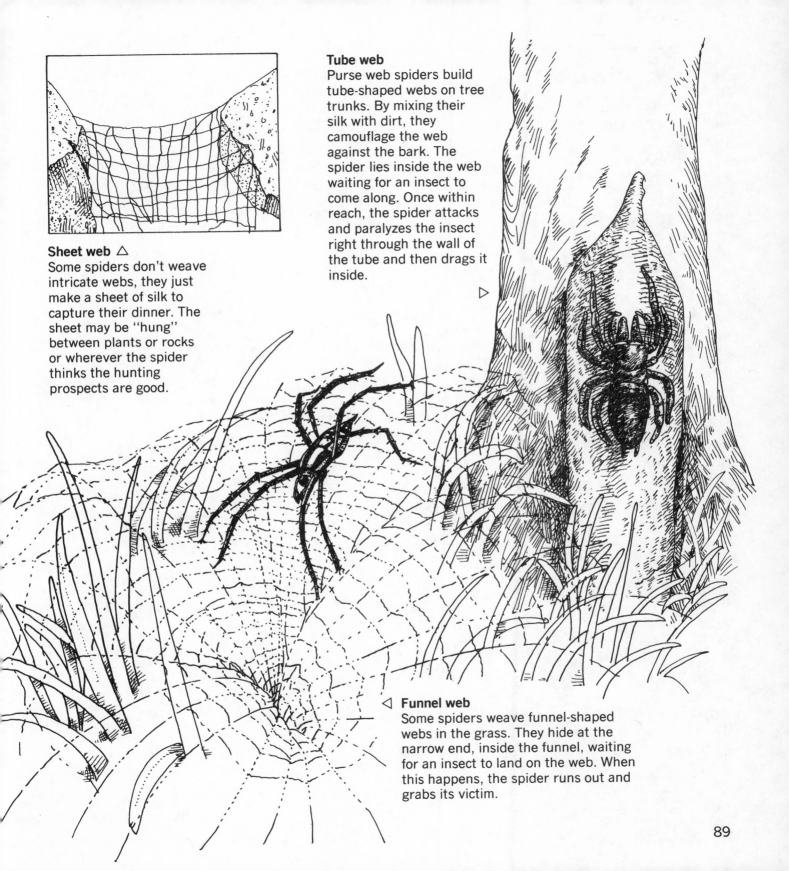

Sheet web △
Some spiders don't weave intricate webs, they just make a sheet of silk to capture their dinner. The sheet may be "hung" between plants or rocks or wherever the spider thinks the hunting prospects are good.

Tube web
Purse web spiders build tube-shaped webs on tree trunks. By mixing their silk with dirt, they camouflage the web against the bark. The spider lies inside the web waiting for an insect to come along. Once within reach, the spider attacks and paralyzes the insect right through the wall of the tube and then drags it inside.

▷

◁ **Funnel web**
Some spiders weave funnel-shaped webs in the grass. They hide at the narrow end, inside the funnel, waiting for an insect to land on the web. When this happens, the spider runs out and grabs its victim.

Web watching . . .

Why not invite a spider to spin for you, and see how it's really done?

You'll need:
a forked branch
a large glass container, like a 4-L
    (4-quart) mustard jar
a piece of fine screening
an elastic band
insects
a plant mister with water

1. Place the branch in the container.
2. Collect an orb-weaver spider, such as a common garden spider, from the wild and gently place it on the branch.
3. Cover the container with the screen and secure it with the elastic.

4. Watch as the spider spins its web. Once the web is built, add a couple of live flying insects, such as flies or mosquitoes, and watch the action.

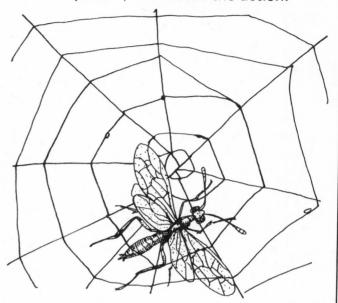

5. Spray the web with a fine mist of water to provide your spider with some moisture.

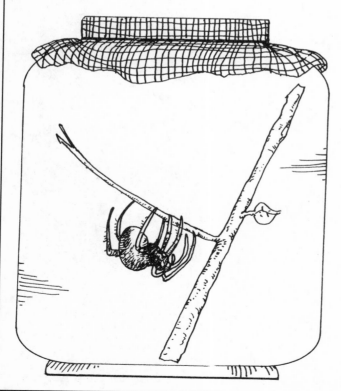

6. Let your spider go after a day or so.

. . . *and collecting*

Unlike birds' nests, spider webs can be collected with no danger to their owners. Spiders rebuild their webs frequently and quickly. You can collect different shapes or patterns of webs, or do crafts using spider webs.

You'll need:
a can of clear spray lacquer
a piece of heavy black paper
scissors
clear plastic wrap

1. Locate a good spider web.
2. Make sure the spider is gone, then spray the web lightly with lacquer three or four times until it is stiff.

3. Place a piece of heavy paper right under the web.
4. Very carefully cut the strands that attach the web to its supports.

5. Have your paper ready to catch the web as it comes loose.

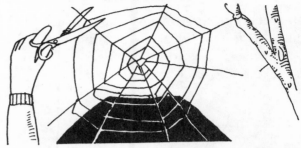

6. Spray another light coating of lacquer on to the paper to make the web stick.

7. Cover your web and paper with clear plastic wrap if you want to keep it for a collection.
8. You can also use different colours of spray paint to make colourful spider web pictures.

More insect impostors

When you're hunting for insects, you'll probably turn up a lot of insect impostors. That's great because non-insects are neat too. Here are a few to keep your eye out for.

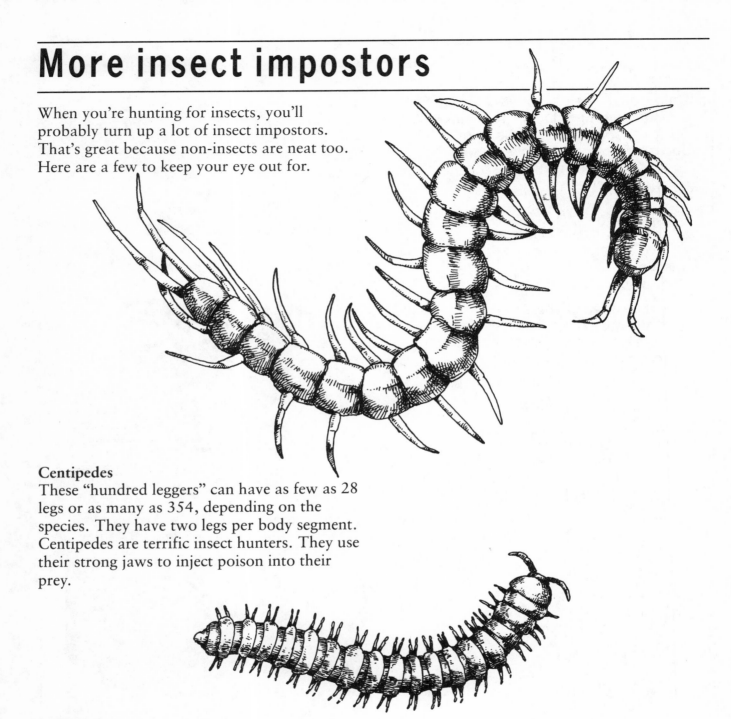

Centipedes
These "hundred leggers" can have as few as 28 legs or as many as 354, depending on the species. They have two legs per body segment. Centipedes are terrific insect hunters. They use their strong jaws to inject poison into their prey.

Millipede
Although its name means 1000 feet, it doesn't really have that many. Each segment has four legs so the longer the body is, the more legs it has.

Harvestmen
You probably call them daddy-long-legs. These spider-like creatures are harmless but they may give off a bad smell if handled carelessly.

Mites
Where can you find mites? There are millions of mites in a hectare (acre) of top soil, feeding on decaying plant and animal matter. Tiny, bright red water mites are often seen swimming around in ponds and marshes.

Pill bug
Sometimes confused with the similar looking wood louse or sow bug, this small armadillo-like creature has seven pairs of legs. When frightened, it rolls into a ball, like a hard, black pill. Sow bugs don't roll up.

Scorpion
Scorpions have super stingers on their tails. A quick flick of the end of its tail can leave you with a painful mark.

INDEX